Costing the Earth

How to Fix Finance to Save the Planet

Eric Archambeau

First published in 2022 by Eric Archambeau
in partnership with whitefox publishing

www.wearewhitefox.com

ISBN Paperback 978-1-915036-48-3
Also available as an ebook
ISBN 978-1-915036-49-0

Figure 1: München, Deutsches Museum, Kalorienzähler: Bundesarchiv, Bild 102-14096 / CC-BY-SA 3.0.

Figure 2: *Village Fair at Hoboken*, c. 1559. Rosenwald Collection.

Designed and typeset by seagulls.net
Project management by whitefox
Printed and bound by CPI Group (UK) Ltd, Croydon CR0 4YY

Contents

Preface

Studying statistical thermodynamics at UC Berkeley, and 'fault tolerant' computing at Stanford University in the early 1980s, was not, perhaps, the most conventional of routes into the world of agriculture and food. However, these studies, alongside my early entrepreneurial journey in data-mining and game theory, made me a believer in the need for strong data analysis to inform better decision-making. And whether we're talking about regulators, investors or consumers, fully informed decisions are sorely needed these days, most particularly when it comes to climate-related policymaking and consumption choices.

It was my later career as a venture capitalist that helped me spot the recent trends in biotech, precision farming and food logistics development that are, together, ushering in a new era in the agri-food technology sector. While these agri-food innovations rarely trouble the front pages, news bulletins and social media (no doubt because they are the wrong sort of news, to paraphrase Steven Pinker), they have the capacity to alter the trajectories of several deadly trends: by drastically lowering global greenhouse gas emissions, reducing freshwater shortages due to human activities, halting the catastrophic collapse of biodiversity and putting an end to the fast-growing obesity epidemic.

Yet these new technologies, even if brought to market by unstoppable, purpose-driven entrepreneurs, might very well miss broad market acceptance if nothing is done to change the way we measure and account for the true cost of the way we do business today. Without a complete, 360-degree view of the total costs to society of maintaining incumbent corporations' products and services at their current level of carbon emissions, water, forests and soil degradation – as well as the social and health tolls exacted on human populations – this new wave of start-ups may never gather the required escape velocity to reach full financial and market momentum.

This book is an attempt to explain why shifting to impact investing practices is so urgent, as it is perhaps the only way to allow this new generation of agri-food tech companies to find the required financial backing to challenge the sector's incumbents, while there is still time for our planet to recover – and for us all to enjoy great food that should not cost the earth.

Eric Archambeau
Brussels

Introduction

At the tail end of 2002, after two decades in Silicon Valley as a technology entrepreneur and, later, a venture capital investor, I was approached by Gabriel Hawawini, then the dean of INSEAD, the international graduate business school, to teach a course in entrepreneurship. I readily accepted and soon the two of us were having lunch together at their Fontainebleau campus, near Paris. What exactly, asked Gabriel, did I want to teach? I responded by saying that while I could certainly offer some real-world insight into starting, financing and scaling fast-growth companies, as well as tackling thorny turnarounds, I actually wanted to focus on something quite different: namely, how the next generation of entrepreneurs would, in addition to all of the above, also need to know how to align the values and mission of a company with its operations. I was convinced that we were on the cusp of an entirely new era, and not offering a class on social entrepreneurship – although it was a relatively new topic at the time – would soon be seen as a major oversight for a school of INSEAD's stature.

While he agreed with the premise, Gabriel was skeptical that there would be much take-up from students. So, I suggested we conduct a survey. The result was a landslide: 75 per cent of students said they would be interested in taking a class on an introduction to social entrepreneurship. I was given the green light to create and teach an elective course on the topic, which in a matter of days became oversubscribed.

My time in the Valley had taught me that times were changing fast and I'd long had a hunch that, as they inherit the world from their parents, the next generation of business founders and entrepreneurs wouldn't care just about the bottom line, but would want to drive purpose alongside profit. More particularly they would see business as a means with which to change the world. They flatly rejected the notion that 'doing good' and having a positive impact on people and the planet should be left to foundations and charities, invariably set up in the twilight of successful business careers, and often devoid of genuine concern for social and environmental issues.

Nevertheless, I wasn't naive. A huge gulf remained back then between the business world and the non-profit sector in particular, and it was especially evident in France. While we were launching the INSEAD course, we invited a group of heads of French non-profit organizations – known as 'associations' in France, which are largely funded by the state – to come to a meeting about participating in our course for free. We thought it would be a great opportunity for some cross-pollination between the business and non-profit worlds; a bridge-building exercise, which might not only boost understanding of social entrepreneurship, but also encourage some high-flying INSEAD students to work for associations, or found their own.

That turned out to be hopelessly optimistic. Quite a few association executives turned up and were vocally and aggressively anti-business from the get-go. In raised voices they told us they had nothing to learn from financiers, and didn't need 'capitalists like us' to tell them what to do. They claimed all work in the social and environmental fields should be underwritten by the state, and that money from successful entrepreneurs was inherently tainted. They went on to spout conspiracy theories, which I can only describe as the Bill Gates COVID-19 vaccine theories[1] of their day. We were told that we had a hidden agenda, and were interested only in eventually profiting from them … And so it went on until they left the meeting, slamming the door behind them. Of the ten or so association leaders in that meeting, only a couple would give us any kind of a hearing.

That experience – which I can only liken to an ice-cold shower – brought home to us how far apart the worlds of business and non-profits had become. Mistrust was manifest and, if I'm honest, mutual, while the very notion that we might want the same outcomes was not just fanciful to them, but an affront.

The chasm between capitalism on the one hand and social and environmental concerns on the other developed in the mid-twentieth century. Few articulated, or arguably encouraged, it more explicitly than the Nobel Prize-winning economist Milton Friedman. In his seminal 1970 essay for the *New York Times Magazine* entitled 'A Friedman Doctrine',[2] he argued that a company has no social responsibility to the public or society or the environment: '…there is one and only one social responsibility of business – to use its resources and engage in activities designed to increase its profits …'

In a post-war context, where communism and socialism – often used interchangeably – were viewed as twin existential threats to the American way of life (it's notable that Friedman refers disparagingly to 'preaching pure and unadulterated socialism' in his essay), the Friedman worldview held sway from boardrooms to presidential and prime ministerial offices. His ten-part TV series *Free to Choose* was broadcast in the UK in early 1980, and according to the Margaret Thatcher Foundation, he was held in such reverence that '(Thatcher's) government approached his arrival pre-screening almost as a state visit'.[3]

He went on to advise both Thatcher, the US Treasury and Ronald Reagan, while his belief in free trade, open markets, privatization, a lean state, limits to government intervention and deregulation had a global impact, through the US and Britain's then political domination of the World Bank, the International Monetary Fund (IMF) and the precursor to the World Trade Organization (WTO), the General Agreement on Tariffs and Trade (GATT).[4]

In many ways the 1980s were the Friedman doctrine writ large. And the economist's pomp extended deep into the following decade, too, as illustrated by the 1997 Statement on Corporate Governance from the Business Roundtable.[5] Parroting Friedman (without quoting him directly), the association of CEOs from America's leading companies declared: 'The paramount duty of management and of boards of directors is to the corporation's stockholders; the interests of other stakeholders are relevant as a derivative of the duty to stockholders. The notion that the board must somehow balance the interests of stockholders against the interests of other stakeholders fundamentally misconstrues the role of directors.'

Disconnection

There were a number of factors which drew the 'Friedman era' finally and decisively to a close. Among them was the Great Recession of 2008–10 – a direct consequence of deregulation of the finance sector – which brought the sense of disconnection between corporations and their impact on the wider world into sharp focus. Another was the slow but growing drumbeat of urgency surrounding the environmental movement. While the climate protests in Copenhagen in 2009,[6] and in New York City[7] five years later, helped bring global warming to TV screens and newspaper front pages, it was perhaps Al Gore more than anyone else who propelled the green agenda from the activist fringes to centre stage.

As US VP in 1997 Gore had helped broker the Kyoto Protocol to curb greenhouse gas emissions. Then, in the aftermath of his rancorous defeat to George W. Bush in 2000, he took to crisscrossing the globe to deliver his famous slide-show presentation on global warming to over a thousand audiences worldwide.

I happened to catch Gore's talk at TED in 2005 in Monterey, California, and saw audience members challenge him directly to find a more impactful way to deliver his message than a slide deck that they considered simply too detailed and, bluntly, too long. It turned out that one of the participants in a working breakfast meeting that I attended during that conference had just started a new documentary film production company with the goal of producing entertainment with socially relevant themes. That individual was Jeff Skoll, a technology executive whose early tenure at eBay made him wealthy and enabled him to focus on his true passion: filmmaking. Skoll offered to help Gore, and the Oscar-winning movie *An Inconvenient Truth* was born out of this serendipitous encounter, airing a year later to great acclaim. The film also changed the game in terms of global awareness of the issues raised, with the climatologist Professor Steve Quiring arguing that it 'had a much greater impact on public opinion and public awareness of global climate change than any scientific paper or report'.[8]

It would, however, take another decade for the Paris Agreement to be signed in 2016, and two further years for the notion that business/finance do not exist in a bubble – and cannot be separated from their social and environmental impact – to filter through to the constituency with the greatest ability to drive change: business leaders and boardrooms.

Slamming the door on Friedman

A watershed moment finally arrived in 2018, when BlackRock CEO Larry Fink's Letter to CEOs, entitled 'A sense of purpose',[9] turned Friedman-era orthodoxies on their head. Fink, whose firm managed over $6 trillion at the time, committed to a new model of 'sustainable growth', declaring that 'to prosper over time, every company must not only deliver financial performance, but also show how it makes a positive contribution to society. Companies must benefit all of their stakeholders, including shareholders, employees, customers, and the communities in which they operate.'

Slamming the door on Friedman – and, if we're honest, sensing a sea change among their clients – he added that 'a company's ability to manage environmental, social and governance matters demonstrates the leadership and good governance that is so essential to sustainable growth, which is why we are increasingly integrating these issues into our investment process'.

After that the floodgates opened. Each prior version of the Business Roundtable (BRT) had endorsed principles of shareholder primacy. In a 360-degree reversal, in August 2019 the association published a statement signed by more than 180 leading CEOs, which redefined the purpose of a corporation away from shareholder primacy to include a commitment to all stakeholders.[10] Among its specific declarations, the BRT pledged: 'We respect the people in our communities and protect the environment by embracing sustainable practices across our businesses.'

To be clear about how big a volte-face this was: up until that point corporations had been under a legal obligation to maximize financial returns to investors. Indeed, a corporation's board of directors could be sued for considering external factors such as the environmental impact of its factories or the social impact on surrounding communities of its commercial or marketing activities.

The notion that corporations would from then on also be values-driven, taking into account the impact they are having on their employees, the environment and their customers was predictably met with a barrage of derision from some quarters. Citing examples of the recent leadership behaviours of Boeing, General Motors and Amazon, former US Labor Secretary Robert Reich, who served under President Clinton, memorably dismissed the Roundtable's pronouncement as 'the second biggest con of 2019' (after Donald Trump) and urged readers 'not to believe a word of it'.[11]

Major inflection point

While retaining a healthy dose of scepticism is essential where the conduct of big business is concerned – a report from ShareAction in March 2020[12] found that thirty-eight of the world's seventy-five largest asset managers including BlackRock, Vanguard and State Street scored badly on responsible investing – we must also acknowledge that pivoting away from shareholder primacy marked a major inflection point.

Its context, too, is crucial, coming as it did in response to a significant shift in public opinion with consumers increasingly holding businesses to account for their impact on, and support for, issues around social justice and the environment. A recent Kantar survey,[13] for example, found that 68 per cent of US consumers expect brands to be explicit about their values and take an unambiguous stance on social issues (the numbers were notably highest among African Americans and millennials).

Yet this has become about more than making a stand. Empowered and emboldened by social media, campaigning consumers, especially millennials and those from Generation Z – through youth activist movements such as the Greta Thunberg-inspired Fridays for Future[14] – believe they can now directly affect change. As the consumers, employees, founders and politicians of the future, they know only too well that corporate bosses are nothing if not pragmatic and, when fearful of a hashtag-led backlash, will ultimately act in their own self-interest.

Emmanuel Faber, who joined my firm Astanor Ventures as a partner in the summer of 2021, and was until recently the CEO of food giant Danone and a leading global proponent of 'responsible capitalism', says this groundswell of opinion among younger consumers that large companies in particular must exist for a purpose has in effect jolted corporations into behaving more responsibly, in large part because new mission-driven start-ups had begun to chip away at their bottom line.

'What I saw with the food revolution over the last ten years was that smaller companies, start-ups, were eating into the pie of the larger ones. That ended, at least temporarily, with the pandemic in 2020, but before that every year globally half a point to one point of market share was taken from large multinational companies and brands by smaller insurgent brands. That was a wake-up call to me that if we didn't act by self-disrupting, by explaining our mission and our commitments, showing who the people are behind the brand, and acting authentically and responsibly, then we were going to be on the wrong side of the story at the end of the day.'

I also experienced this shift first-hand as chairman of the Jamie Oliver Food Foundation, which was set up by the campaigning celebrity British chef to improve food education and reduce the impact of diet-related disease. With hindsight, we were probably too early in trying to change people's eating habits. Few were ready back in 2005 to embrace healthier school meals or curbing sugar intake by taxing carbonated sodas. Poor-quality diets – low in nutrients and high in processed foods, with ever-increasing amounts of added sugars, combined with sugary drinks – have proliferated in the years since, among children and teenagers in particular. As a result, child obesity rates worldwide continued to climb over the ensuing decade, so that by 2019, more than 91 million schoolchildren globally were defined as not just overweight, but obese,[15] and on a near-certain path to developing type 2 diabetes by young adulthood – if they weren't already diabetics.

However, while we fell short of our ambitions in those areas, we were able to have a lasting impact. A TV campaign fronted by Jamie exposed the horrific conditions of battery-farmed chickens to a mainstream audience, leading to Unilever, makers of Hellmann's mayonnaise, to switch to free-range eggs, and moving hens out of cages (although Unilever claimed the change was already in the works).[16] We achieved this not because Jamie was a nice guy (although he is) and it was the right thing to do, but because – with his huge public profile and, later, millions of followers on social media – the processed food industry couldn't afford to ignore or antagonize him.

Such campaigns have, if anything, become even more powerful and incisive today. During the pandemic in the UK, Manchester United's Marcus Rashford scored a similar victory when he locked horns with the government over the provision of free school meals for children from deprived homes.[17] Boris Johnson's government had initially said it would not provide vouchers over the 2020 summer holidays for the 1.3 million children in England who were in receipt of free school meals during term time, arguing that it had already offered families higher welfare payments due to the pandemic instead. Not only was the government forced into an embarrassing climb-down after public (media and social media) pressure, but Rashford ended up being awarded an MBE for his campaign to boot.

And it's not just celebrities with legions of followers who are holding governments and giant corporations to account. Employees, too, now routinely expect their bosses' values to reflect their own. A 2021 survey from Fidelity[18] found that 87 per cent of millennials, when considering a future employer, believe 'it's important for (them) to work for a company that engages in corporate social responsibility'. By comparison 71 per cent of people from Generation X and 64 per cent of baby boomers agreed with that statement.

And this is especially true within Big Tech. Whether it was Google employees successfully protesting the company's involvement in a Pentagon AI drone imagery project,[19] Salesforce staffers petitioning bosses over its contract with US Customs and Border Patrol[20] or Amazon workers ignoring corporate policy to attack the company for failing to meet the challenge of the climate crisis,[21] employees are unafraid to speak out publicly in a way never seen before.

It's hitting the mark, too. Microsoft, for example, announced that it would go carbon neutral by 2030[22] after a run of embarrassing employee protests[23] triggered by the company's alleged 'complicity' in the climate crisis.

Making an impact

While social issues are of critical importance, of course, in this book I shall focus primarily on the global movement coalescing around the climate emergency, and in particular the growing realization that returning to a sustainable path for our planet and our descendants demands the urgent decarbonization of the global economy. As Bill Gates argued in his 2020 book *How to Avoid a Climate Emergency*, failure to get to net zero is not an option, while getting there will require nothing less than a reboot of capitalism itself, where financial support is redirected away from companies and projects negatively impacting the planet and its inhabitants and channelled instead towards those who are developing the technology and behavioural breakthroughs that are needed.

Since the Business Roundtable's shift away from shareholder primacy in 2019, a number of prominent figures in the finance industry have come to support a radically new approach to finance: impact investing. Unlike traditional investing, which centres on financial returns, impact investments have a dual mandate: they seek to generate positive, measurable social and environmental impact *alongside* financial return. And the investments they make are in socially and environmentally purpose-driven companies.

Once niche, impact investing is fast reaching a tipping point and being adopted by the likes of BlackRock's Larry Fink as central to successful fund performance. 'A company cannot achieve long-term profits without embracing purpose and considering the needs of a broad range of stakeholders,' he wrote in his February 2020 letter to CEOs. 'A fundamental reshaping of finance' was needed, he said.

Later that year, speaking at Bloomberg Sustainable Investment Summit, Peter Harrison, the group CEO of Schroders PLC, said[24] – in what I believe may well turn out to be a defining moment for the future of impact investing: 'Asset managers need to be more aggressive in tracking the impact of environmental and societal events on corporate earnings and their investments …

'We are at a transformational moment in the history of the asset-management industry, and while investors once focused only on profits, we are at a new juncture and we need to go a step further,' Harrison added. 'Investors can use "big data" to get a clearer picture of externalities that affect a company's bottom line.'

Unlike the integration of ESG criteria into investment decision-making – which focuses on the environmental, social and governance practices of the internal-facing operations of a given company and often amounts to little more than virtue-signalling – impact investing is all about the external influence (i.e. impact) the company has on society and the environment via the products and services that it produces. An 'impact company' is specifically making goods and services aimed at solving important environmental and social problems. Where ESG is about how companies *go about* doing what they do, impact investing is about *what they actually do*.

From the climate crisis to the excesses of factory farming and the obesity epidemic, a gathering storm, by orders of magnitude more lethal than COVID-19, is heading slowly but inexorably humanity's way. As the turbulence approaches, the stakes continue to rise and the window for action closes, impact investing is finally getting the attention it deserves and could – and, I will argue, must – become a baseline for the next generation of asset owners and managers.

Many questions have yet to be answered. If as Peter Harrison states 'not all profits are created equally', then how do we meaningfully gauge impact-related performance? What types of problems are impact companies primarily aiming to solve? And how do you screen for impact in the first place?

As with many new fields, understanding what to look for and how to look for it requires an entirely fresh approach. New tools and frameworks are essential. So is a new map. And drawing that new map is the purpose of this book.

A brief history of humanity's impact on Earth

and the collapse of our current model

Soil's backstory

Humanity's pervasive smash-and-grab attitude to Earth's finite
resources – from food to hydrocarbons to soil – has ended
some civilizations and brought others to the brink. Of these,
the role of soil is often the least well understood. It had long
been argued that soil erosion resulting from deforestation[1] was
a major factor in the demise of civilizations around the world,
ranging from the ancient societies of Neolithic Europe, classical
Greece and Rome, to the southern United States and Central
America. However, in his acclaimed book *Dirt: The Erosion of
Civilization*, author and geomorphologist Professor David R.
Montgomery makes the case that rather than the axe (the
symbol of deforestation), the real culprit was in fact the plough
that followed, as tillage fundamentally altered the balance
between soil production and erosion.[2]

I first became conscious of the widespread degradation of topsoil caused by agricultural practices thanks to Charles (Chuck) de Liedekerke, a young entrepreneur who left investment banking to launch Soil Capital, one of the very first start-ups to promote regenerative agriculture. Having mentored Chuck for a few years, I became the first investor in Soil Capital when it launched in 2013. Later, in July 2019, I invited Professor Montgomery to a soil regeneration workshop that our firm Astanor Ventures organized in the Loire Valley together with Soil Capital. We had a fascinating few days, during which we exchanged views on soil erosion and regenerative farming practices.

When I spoke to him a couple of years later for this book, he said: 'There are not many natural ecosystems that have vast expanses of bare soil at the surface. Nature tends to clothe herself in plants, and the plough has been popular because it's really good at weed control. What could be better weed control than basically ploughing under the existing vegetation, having a blank slate and starting over with what you want to grow? So, there's a rationale behind it.

'And while the downside accumulates over time, the upside is quick: it benefits the farmer this year not only in terms of weed control, but also with tillage you accelerate the breakdown of soil organic matter, which enhances nutrient cycling. So, you get a little burst of fertility and productivity out of the soil. But it comes at the expense of the long-term fertility of the soil. And that's the real conundrum, because what the plough does is it leaves the soil bare and vulnerable to erosion by rainfall and blowing winds. And if that happens often enough, for long enough, you can literally strip the soil off a landscape,' he told me.

'You lose the best stuff first'

'One of the awkward things about soil and soil erosion, in particular, is that you lose the best stuff first, because the topsoil is really the font of fertility,' Montgomery continued. 'It's where the organisms live that cycle things, that mix the elements that come out of rotting rock particles and decaying organic matter – and that life repurposes those elements in ways that can be taken up by new life. Soil erosion skims the best stuff off the top first. And if it's sustained for long enough – if we erode soils faster than we replace or rebuild them – you can literally run out of them. It just takes longer than most people are accustomed to thinking about things. You notice the changes over a lifetime, or over the lifetime of a civilization.'

He expanded: 'The basic problem with tillage, and with the plough – and the reason I've argued that the plough has been more destructive than the axe, over thousands of years – is that trees grow back pretty fast. If you just come in and cut the forest down and let it grow back, you get this little burst of erosion, but it heals itself. Disturbance is a natural phenomenon in many ecosystems, and if you just cut the forest down once and let it grow back … I won't say there's no impact, but, integrated over time, it's marginal. If, on the other hand, after you cut the forest down, you keep ploughing the surface so that it's bare and vulnerable to wind or rain on an annual basis, it only takes decades to centuries for that to really integrate into lost fertility and productivity of the land. And that's the story of civilization after civilization around the world in terms of agriculture being a beneficial short-term endeavour and having detrimental long-term impacts.'

Montgomery went on to cite the example of Palouse, in eastern Washington State, which saw about five feet of soil eroded in the half-century between 1911 and 1961, amounting to about a foot a decade, or an inch a year. 'The Palouse region is the semi-arid dry half of the state of Washington. And what's happened there is you had these fragile soils that are also very fertile, but didn't have much water naturally. When the rivers got dammed and irrigation became a common thing in eastern Washington, agriculture really expanded, and tillage was the way to do it. But over the last century, that reliance on tillage has meant the Palouse has lost roughly 50 per cent of its topsoil. That's a pretty shocking number to a geologist like myself, because if you can burn through half the supply of something in a century, that's a pretty scary pace if you forecast out the ability to farm for the next century or the century beyond that.'

The arrival of the plough broke up the root system of the native grasslands, which left the soil exposed to the next big windstorm, Montgomery said. He described places in the Palouse where you can see an almost cliff-like effect at the edge of a field, where one field's been ploughed and the other field hasn't been ploughed for half a century, and there's literally feet of difference on the two sides due to topsoil loss. 'Yet when you look at it on a daily basis, it's pretty hard for the human mind to connect that whiff of dust blowing off of a field one afternoon to the long-term loss that lowers the whole landscape,' he said.

'Close to extinction'

Over the past 150,000 years or so, human existence has always been particularly intertwined with available food supply. As the investor and co-founder of GMO Capital Jeremy Grantham described in his 2011 essay 'Time to Wake Up: Days of Abundant Resources and Falling prices Are Over Forever':[3] 'A good rainy season, and food, is plentiful, and births are plentiful. A few tough years, and the population shrinks way back. It seems likely, in fact, that our species came close to extinction at least once and perhaps several times.'

I recall Montgomery telling us at the workshop that if you look at the geology and the archaeology of societies around the world over the last 10,000 years, roughly the window of agriculture, there's a consistent story: societies that have a surplus of healthy fertile soil relative to their population can grow, and grow aggressively and productively, by expanding farming both in scale and scope. Whereas if a society has a large population and a diminishing supply of healthy, fertile land, they are putting a squeeze on their ability to sustain themselves over the long run.

Since the ancient Egyptians – the first civilization to practise agriculture at scale thanks to the Blue and White Nile's summer floods, which refertilized land along the river basin[4] – soil has thus borne the brunt of humanity's inextinguishable instinct for survival. In his writing, Montgomery argues that with the rise of mechanized agriculture, soil was increasingly viewed as an industrial commodity to be used and, potentially, used up. The net effect of that has been nothing short of catastrophic for the planet.

This is also one of the foundational premises behind the regenerative agriculture movement. Soil Capital, one of the movement's pioneers, has been teaching the farmers that work with them to look at the profit and loss equation of farming differently, whereby the full array of inputs and outputs are factored in so that the farmer can see the complete picture of their farm's economic activity, rather than the partial version they had before.

When one considers all the expensive inputs into modern agriculture – fuel for tractors, ever-increasing fertilizer needs, ever-more sophisticated pesticides, patented seeds and so on – the margins left for the farmer become razor-thin, Montgomery told me. 'But losing a little bit of soil doesn't directly cost the farmer money in any given year, which is how soil has become treated as essentially the lowest cost input into the agricultural production process. Because once you own land, your marginal cost for continuing to work the soil is minimal. And so it tends to get discounted in terms of conservation.

'Soil erosion ends up then generally being deprioritized as a major concern,' he said. 'Yet if you think about the problem of maintaining agriculture on a societal scale, over generations, then the loss of fertility and the loss of the soil becomes a critical issue. Because as soon as you're looking out over the long run, even a small rate of soil loss, given time, will eventually add up to big changes.'

Soil erosion, moreover, is only one strand of the story.

In August 2019, a report by the Intergovernmental Panel on Climate Change (IPCC),[5] the global body that assesses the state of scientific knowledge related to climate change, spelled out the indispensable role land management plays in the climate system. 'Agriculture, forestry and other types of land use account for around a quarter of human greenhouse gas (GHG) emissions,' said Jim Skea, co-chair of IPCC Working Group III, which focuses on climate change mitigation, including by assessing methods for reducing GHG emissions.[6] 'At the same time natural land processes absorb carbon dioxide equivalent to almost a third of carbon dioxide emissions from fossil fuels and industry.'

Humanity is now caught in a vicious cycle in its use of land, the IPCC scientists continued: 'When land is degraded, it becomes less productive, restricting what can be grown and reducing the soil's ability to absorb carbon. This exacerbates climate change, while climate change in turn exacerbates land degradation in many different ways.'

Hydrocarbons

Sustenance aside, most of humanity's development – population growth, economic and scientific advances – has been driven by the progressive discovery, development and exploitation of increasingly powerful energy resources. The principal energy sources of antiquity, for example, were derived directly from the sun: human and animal muscle power, wood, flowing water and wind.[7] The industrial revolution began in 1750 with stationary wind- and water-powered technologies.

Today, it's easy to forget that until the eighteenth century we relied exclusively on wood for producing the charcoal used in making steel, which was critical to improving machinery – a key driver of progress. But in the eighteenth century the world started to run out of wood and the Western world would likely have slid into oblivion had it not been for the discovery of hydrocarbon fuels – a high-density storage of the sun's energy formed by millions of years' worth of compressed, decayed vegetable and animal matter – specifically coal in the nineteenth century and oil since the twentieth century, increasingly followed by natural gas. Furthermore, coal's higher combustion temperatures enabled the making of more and better steel that led to the production of more efficient tools and energy transformation processes, without which the development of heavy industry would not have been possible.

Extracting and using hydrocarbons over the past two centuries, from c.1800 to 2020, enabled humanity to remove the barriers to rapid population growth through improved agricultural yields and scientific progress to allow for unprecedented advances in transportation, sanitation, healthcare and industrial productivity.[8] In their paper 'Hydrocarbons and the evolution of human culture', academics Charles Hall et al. estimate that 'the global use of hydrocarbons for fuel by humans has increased nearly 800-fold since 1750 and about 12-fold in the twentieth century'.[9]

Our advanced industrial and technological societies are still underpinned by hydrocarbons today. Without them, energy-guzzling rockets, AI-based software and crypto-currencies would not be remotely possible. According to one estimate published in Nature,[10] data centres/server farms alone use an estimated 200-terawatt hours (TWh) each year globally: more than the entire national energy consumption of a mid-sized country.

The Information and Communications Technology (ICT) ecosystem as a whole – covering devices, mobile phone networks and TVs – accounts for more than 2 per cent of global emissions, only slightly less than the global aviation industry. Worryingly, one model reported by Nature predicts that by the time a child born today reaches their teens, electricity use by ICT could exceed 20 per cent of the global total, with data centres accounting for about a third of that.

Indeed, hydrocarbon extraction and burning has come at a terrible, and intensifying, cost. Since the start of the industrial revolution, human-caused carbon emissions into the atmosphere 'rose slowly to about 5 billion tons per year in the mid-20th century before skyrocketing to more than 35 billion tons per year by the end of the century', according to the US scientific and regulatory agency the National Oceanic and Atmospheric Administration (NOAA).[11] Today human activity across the planet, including agriculture and land use, results in an additional 51 billion tons of greenhouse gases (GHGs)[12] being released into the atmosphere (although I should note that number can vary, depending on what exactly is counted.) And, with over 80 per cent of primary energy demand still being met by fossil fuels,[13] there's little sign of global emissions dropping anytime soon. As I write these words, the world is convulsed in an energy shock, providing a stark reminder of the scale of the task ahead of us. 'Since May (2021) the price of a basket of oil, coal and gas has soared by 95%,' according to *The Economist*. 'Britain, the host of the (COP26 Glasgow) summit, has turned its coal-fired power stations back on, American petrol prices have hit $3 a gallon, blackouts have engulfed China and India, and Vladimir Putin has reminded Europe that its supply of fuel relies on Russian goodwill.' No wonder, then, that we are still in the very thick of the so-called Anthropocene era, defined by *National Geographic* as 'an unofficial unit of geological time, used to describe the most recent period of Earth's history when human activity started to have a significant impact on the planet's climate and ecosystems'.[14]

Indeed, it was only in the past couple of decades and the growing – first, scientific, then popular – realization that the burning of fossil fuels was causing lasting change to our climate that renewable and sustainable alternatives to hydrocarbon energy were pursued in earnest. Yet the push to build, expand

and maintain renewable energy sources globally before the clock runs down, and we run out of fossil fuels – a race we cannot afford to lose – will largely be powered, by definition, by hydrocarbons. (Especially since the Fukushima disaster of 2011, which has led to a decline of trust in nuclear power, the only surefire way for mankind to bridge the gap; more on this later.) If we run out of accessible, affordable and GHG-emissions-limited hydrocarbons by that time and fall short in that mission, modern life as we know it, if not our civilization itself, will once again be teetering on the brink.

Some dismiss this as alarmism, arguing that humanity's ingenuity will lead us out of trouble or we'll get steadily better at producing more and consuming less. To them I say our track record rather suggests the opposite: every time we find a way to save energy on one thing, we discover new ways to consume more on something else. Bitcoin is a prime example. Similarly, as more of our lives – and critical infrastructure – shift online, the demand for energy-devouring data centres, so artificial intelligence and quantum computing, not to mention cyber defences, ramps up ad infinitum.

Food

As I've described, the battle to maintain a stable atmosphere on Earth – one that keeps our species alive and in harmony with the rest of the planet – before we run out of cheap energy sources is far from over and may yet not end well for humanity. There is a path for success, but it is obstacle-strewn and narrowing fast. First politicians will have to expend unprecedented political capital and act decisively against vested interests to put incentives and regulatory frameworks in place to curb global warming, and limit it to the 'well below 2, preferably to 1.5 degrees Celsius' pledged at the COP21 Paris Agreement.[15] That's starting, slowly, to happen, but grandstanding goals and objectives on their own are just that.

Next, we need to zero in on the right areas. Contrary to most people's belief, the biggest contributors to CO_2 emissions are not the sectors that may first spring to mind. Heavy industries have been on a fast track to transformation for a while now, and energy use in the sector – encompassing, among other things, iron and steel, chemicals and petrochemicals, food, tobacco and paper production – account for around 30 per cent of global GHGs (energy use within industry accounts for about 24 per cent; the remaining 5 per cent comes directly from industrial processes such as the carbon dioxide produced as a by-product of cement production and GHGs that result from chemical and petrochemical manufacturing).[16] CO_2 capture and recycling systems are being adopted that are curbing such emissions dramatically. For example, new uses and products being developed for captured CO_2 include varieties of concrete, chemicals and fuels.

At around 16 per cent, meanwhile, transportation, often a focal point of political and environmental campaigns – which includes road (responsible for about 12 per cent of the sector's emissions), aviation (2 per cent) and shipping (less than 2 per cent), among other less-polluting modes, but doesn't include emissions from the manufacture of automobiles or other transport equipment – is neither the biggest emitter of CO_2, nor of NO_2 (nitrogen dioxide) and NO_4 (oxide nitrate), and still less of the potent CH_4 (methane). What's more, its share is significantly declining thanks to the rapid electrification of the automobile, truck and logistics industries. It also lags behind the built environment/construction (including energy use in the heating and cooling of residential and commercial buildings) and agri-food/forestry/land use, both of which represent around 20 per cent of CO_2 emissions each (depending on what data you use), plus – in the case of agri-food – an overwhelming majority of the more potent CH_4 and NO_2/NO_4 gas emissions.

Of these, agri-food will be the key focus of this book and is where I believe attention and far greater resources should be directed, not least because it offers very real scope for progress.

First, let's look a little more closely at GHG emissions from global food production. Fossil fuel use and the entire life cycle of food production are heavily intertwined. When taken fully into consideration, modern food systems – which use energy to grow, irrigate, fertilize, harvest, process, package, store, refrigerate, distribute and dispose of or recycle food waste – account for over a quarter (26 per cent) of global GHG emissions.[17] Based on data from Joseph Poore and Thomas Nemecek, published in *Science*,[18] the biggest emitters in the sector break down as follows: livestock and fisheries (31 per cent of food emissions); crop production (27 per cent), land use (24 per cent) and supply chains (18 per cent).

Furthermore, not only is the agri-food sector one of the single leading GHG emitters, but agri-food, forestry and land use activities – in aggregate – accounted for 44 per cent of methane (CH_4) and 82 per cent of nitrous oxide (N_2O) emissions from human activities globally during 2007–16, according to the IPCC.[19] It is also the largest user of freshwater, as well as the most significant driver of terrestrial biodiversity loss.

Feeding the five billion

Food, energy, water, human health and life on Earth are a cat's cradle of interconnectedness, which is why we must aim not only for the decarbonization of the global economy, but also to restore water quality and biodiversity, while rebalancing the quality and quantity of the world's food supply. How we finance the revolution for that necessary convergence of goals through impact investing is the purpose of this book – and I believe the only way lasting change can be achieved.

Beside hydrocarbons and the resulting release of GHGs into the atmosphere, our overall demands on nature continue to far exceed its capacity to supply. New technological developments in the renewable energy space, waste management and recycling, clean transportation, green construction and habitat and the vast, sustainable agri-food sector are coming on stream fast and will certainly contribute significantly to mitigating climate change and ocean degradation. But not fast enough. If we are to avoid exceeding the limits of what nature can sustainably provide, while meeting the needs of the human population, even as it grows, then we cannot rely on technology alone: we'll need a fundamental shift in consumption patterns together with regulatory changes and incentives from governments.

What do I mean by that? The EU's ambitious Farm to Fork Strategy[20] laudably aims to accelerate our transition to sustainability, which means having a neutral or positive impact on the environment. It sets out to help mitigate climate change and adapt to its impacts, reverse the loss of biodiversity, ensure food security, nutrition and public health – making sure everyone has access to sufficient, safe, nutritious, sustainable food – while preserving the affordability of food, generating fairer economic returns, fostering competitiveness of the EU supply sector and promoting fair trade. A highly ambitious set of goals. But if they are to be more than that, and we are to achieve, for example, a reduction 'in the use and risk of chemical and more hazardous pesticides by 50% by 2030' – as the strategy calls for – we need to be able to incentivize farmers and food producers to live up to them. And give them the tools with which to do it.

One key example is the future of Europe's Common Agricultural Policy. The European Commission's proposals[21] focus on, among other things, 'setting higher ambitions for environmental and climate action', with nine specific objectives, which include: 'rebalancing the power in the food chain', 'climate change action', 'environmental care' and 'preserving landscapes and biodiversity'. Certainly, this represents, at the EU level, the beginning of a shift away from the idea of farming as a Stakhanovite endeavour – i.e. prioritizing mass production at the expense of environmental considerations. Lasting change should eventually come from technology pioneers. However, in the meantime, while politicians and regulators have established a framework, we are still lacking meaningful measurability. Where, for instance, the strategy calls for a reduction in the use of fertilizers by 2030, how is that measured at the granular level? What's the baseline?

As the global human population continues to grow – from around 7.7 billion today to 9.7 billion in 2050 and predicted by the UN to peak at nearly 11 billion around 2100[22] – these issues are becoming steadily more urgent.

The former CEO of Unilever, Paul Polman, captured the sheer scale of the challenge ahead, in an article co-written by Daniel Servitje, his then co-chair of the G20's Food Security taskforce

B-20, in the *Washington Post*:[23] 'Imagine all the food mankind has produced over the past 8,000 years. Now consider that we need to produce that same amount again – but in just the next 40 years if we are to feed our growing and hungry world.'

And this isn't just about growth (indeed, population growth is slowly levelling off).[24] Rather, it is about how many, as the developing world grows more prosperous, move into the global middle class with its concomitant expectations around food (with their diet moving to intensively produced meat and fish), housing and energy consumption, textiles and consumer goods. Multiplying demand is not, however, being balanced by the necessary reduction in waste, change of diet or drop in consumption. So, in effect the planet is being hit by a double whammy.

Let's be clear: it's certainly not my intention in these pages to shame people into changing their dietary or consumption habits, nor am I calling for certain food categories to be made illegal. My goal is to provide the reader with viable alternatives, which are of similar quality yet entirely sustainable. The only realistic way of doing that is by moving towards the widespread adoption of regenerative agricultural practices[25] – a term which 'describes farming and grazing practices that reverse climate change by rebuilding soil organic matter and restoring degraded soil biodiversity, resulting in both carbon drawdown and improving the water cycle'.

As we'll cover in more detail in Chapter 6, because intensive animal farming is one of the worst offenders when it comes to GHG emissions, and few processes have such a negative effect on biodiversity as wild fisheries, radical innovation is required not only to reduce these impacts but, crucially, also to offer consumers delicious and sustainably grown alternative sources of protein, derived directly from plants from smaller-scale regenerative practices to supplement animal farming. And offer it at the same price.

Redirecting the agri-food sector towards sustainability is only possible through aligning regulatory and government actions with the activities of impact investors to power a new development course.

What do I mean by alignment? Where, say, the Farm to Fork Strategy calls for a reduction in the use of fertilizers and pesticides, and the alternatives are not financially viable, then one option is to incentivize sustainable behaviour through subsidies.

But there's another route, too: to measure the full cost (financial, social, environmental and other externalities) of incumbent practices against cleaner, technology-driven alternatives. And for investors to support those companies.

To do that successfully, however, requires a wholesale change of mindset, and, as we'll see in Chapter 2, a 180-degree reappraisal of our current financial and accounting models, which are no longer fit for purpose.

The big
accounting flaw

A veggie burger isn't what it seems ...

Today a company can legally post profits while entirely
ignoring (or, at best, paying lip service to) the full social and
environmental costs that sourcing, producing, distributing and
consuming its products generate. Let's take the example of a
(fictional) plant-based 'alternative meat' company in London.
When a customer orders a vegetarian burger online, or buys
one in the supermarket, they feel as though they've made
a choice for sustainability, rather than adding to the carbon
footprint of one of the monster fast-food chains (which typically
serve beef from cattle that have been raised indoors in feedlots
on a diet of soya, while often being fed corn to make them
fatten faster).

Now let's say that according to its official accounts the gross
profit margin per unit of that veggie burger for the company is
ostensibly 50 per cent per unit. Sounds pretty healthy, at least
from the producer's perspective. But in reality it's only a partial
picture at best. Once we begin to scratch beneath the surface
of how this supposedly environmentally friendly product got
from soil to supermarket aisle or home delivery, it becomes

clear that the underlying costs to both the environment and human health are substantial – and unsustainable.

On top of that, these same costs are not borne by the company, nor do they appear in its (traditional) profit and loss (P&L) statements, but, rather, it's left for society at large, and to the natural environment, to foot the bill for remedial action and repairs (if any are carried out at all). Indeed, if the full negative impacts of the production of the veggie burger on the planet and society are taken into account, then the company's impact-adjusted profits could very well show a net loss for each burger it serves. So part, or all, of these posted profits are in effect subsidized by borrowing from nature's balance sheet, something that eventually will need to be repaid by future generations.

So, what are the true costs that are ignored in our example?

As is most often the case in Europe, let's say the aforementioned veggie burger has been prepared with soy and other animal-free ingredients, which are sourced from an intensive farming operation in Brazil. We know that alongside logging and cattle ranching, soya production has a history of being linked to deforestation, especially in Brazil, which in 2019 was the world's largest soya exporter, shipping over $26 billion worth of soybeans.[1]

Although Brazil has vastly reduced deforestation rates over the past decade (and at COP26, world leaders pledged to end deforestation by 2030[2]), the Amazon is still being lost at about 6,000 km^2 a year – an area larger than the US state of Delaware.[3]

In January 2020, shortly before the pandemic struck and the cycle of lockdowns began, I visited Brazil at the invitation of Alex Atala, chef extraordinaire and environmental activist. There I met local environmental scientists who shared with me some deeply troubling data: in Europe we import nearly all our soya from Brazil, resulting in the country devoting some 38 million hectares – an area more than twelve times the size of Belgium – to soybean production in 2020–21. Over the 2019–20 season, the country harvested some 122.8 million tons of soybeans.[4] To produce soya at the price that European importers are willing to pay today, Brazil has not only allowed deforestation of the Amazon at scale, but in order to increase yield they are also using enormous quantities of fertilizers and pesticides that stay in their land and water supply long after the soya is harvested.

Even more disturbingly, Brazilian soybean producers are even using chemicals that are banned in Europe, with 52 per cent of the agro-toxins that are used in Brazilian land used for growing soya. In 2019, they used 173,000 tons of glyphosate, half of it for soya export. They also used 12,000 tons of paraquat dichloride, which has been banned in the EU and in the US because of its toxicity, 24,000 tons of atrazine and 27,000 tons of acephate, which are equally dangerous for the local human and animal populations. Once you consider that these chemicals are banned in the very regions where consumers will ultimately buy their seemingly more 'sustainable' product, then it calls into question the very premise of opting for a veggie burger over a beef burger made from an animal raised in a European 'factory farm' (even allowing for the fact that the latter has generated a lot more CO_2 and methane).*

But it gets worse …

––––––––––

* Author's note: if the burger came from an animal raised in a small-scale farm, where it was grass-fed and lived outdoors, the impact on the atmosphere and the environment would be far less even than the veggie burger's. Indeed, if the full cost of the veggie burger was reflected in its price, it would actually make the farmer's burger look much more affordable both for the consumer and the planet.

Infant deaths

A 2019 investigation by Greenpeace revealed that more than 1,200 pesticides and weed killers, including 193 containing chemicals banned in the EU, have been registered in Brazil in just three years under the governments of both Michel Temer and Jair Bolsonaro.[5] Both leaders are reportedly close to Brazil's powerful agribusinesses lobby.[6] Additionally, a number of foreign companies have registered products in Brazil that contain chemicals which would not be approved in their home countries, including German firms Helm and BASF, and China's Adama.

Greenpeace also discovered that half of all products approved since Bolsonaro became president contain active ingredients featured on Pesticide Action Network's list of highly hazardous pesticides, which pose a risk to human health and/or the environment. Furthermore, research from Professor Larissa Mies Bombardi from the University of São Paulo and fellow Brazilian scientists found that soya production in Brazil – to meet growing European and Chinese demand for soya – was causing a death every two and a half days from direct intoxication from agricultural chemicals with alarming incidences among the youngest of the population.[7]

In her report 'The Atlas of Agrotoxins in Brazil and Connection with the European Union', she wrote: 'Our health ministry shows that 343 babies from 0 to 12 months were intoxicated between 2007–2014. What is of even greater concern is that for each case reported there are 50 more that go unreported. This means that in this period we probably had about 17,000 babies intoxicated.'

'We need to rewrite the rules of economics'

All of which casts a markedly different light on our ethically conscious consumers in London, and their decision to opt for a veggie burger on sustainability grounds. While our fictional novel food company can market its products as environmentally friendly at an attractive price point, netting themselves a 50-per-cent gross margin per unit in the process, the true cost of production and health-related issues associated with Brazilian soy served in Europe – which encompasses everything from deforestation to pesticide-intoxication to excessive water irrigation (not to mention the impact of feeding livestock on the same soy) – does not appear in its profit & loss account, or indeed on its balance sheet. Let's be clear: the company in question is not doing anything illegal (at least in terms of local law). Rather, our current 'one-dimensional' accounting system does not enable or impose upon companies the requirement to use the commonly accepted format of the 'double bottom line' (DBL)[8] or 'triple bottom line (TBL) to account for profits alongside social and/or environmental impact – or, as *The Economist* put it, the 'Three Ps: profit, people and the planet'.[9] (The publication goes on to explain that the phrase was first coined in 1994 by John Elkington, who argued that companies should prepare three different (and quite separate) bottom lines: 'One is the traditional measure of corporate profit – the "bottom line" of the profit and loss account. The second is the bottom line of a company's "people account" – a measure in some shape or form of how socially responsible an organization has been throughout its operations. The third is the bottom line of the company's "planet" account – a measure of how environmentally responsible it has been.')

At the moment we can only estimate the costs borne by the Brazilian population and the environment from the country's world-beating soybean industry by laboriously piecing together different sources to build out a fuller picture. Our current accounting model is therefore both dishonest and broken. And ripe for transformation. The good news is that an inflexion point may have been reached recently at COP26 held in Glasgow in November 2021.

For those who may not know it, the IFRS Foundation is an independent, public-interest organization responsible for the governance and oversight of the International Accounting Standards Board. In turn, the Accounting Standards Board is an independent standard-setter that has established over decades international accounting standards, supervised by the international market authorities. It is responsible for the development and promulgation of International Financial Reporting Standards used by companies in more than a hundred countries, including two-thirds of the G20. Almost half of Global Fortune 500 companies report using IFRS Standards.

At COP26, the IFRS Foundation announced the creation of the International Sustainability Standard Board (ISSB) with a mission to establish disclosure standards, which will insert climate, social and governance data into the price and cost of capital mechanisms and will allow capital allocations guided by these data for all capital market participants.[10] In December 2021, Astanor Ventures' partner Emmanuel Faber was named chair of the International Sustainability Standards Board (ISSB).

'This is absolutely the moment where we need to rewrite the rules of economics because we have been extractive, without fully understanding the consequences, when we needed to be regenerative instead,' he says.

'Until we account for the resources, assets and liabilities that are not accounted for in our macro- and microeconomics and accounting systems, these will not accurately reflect the full reality of our economics. They will be flawed in guiding us with appropriate data for relevant decisions on capital allocation. That's true of the macroeconomics accounting of GDP (gross domestic product), and it is true of any of the GAAP (generally accepted accounting principles) systems, simply because companies do not account for the true cost of their operations, their true assets and the true liabilities.' And as I have been arguing in the last two chapters, as long as we lack that data, companies will continue to prioritize short-term efficiency over longer-term resilience.

A close long-time observer and actor of the agri-food industry, Emmanuel says, 'We've now reached the point where, for example, big insurance companies are telling us that a world where temperatures have risen by four degrees is, for sure, an uninsurable one. So, it's very clear to everyone now – to all the key stakeholders – that our P&Ls offer us far too limited and narrow a view, and they need to be much broader.'

(i) Radical Transparency

How, then, do we achieve this breadth? We cannot wait for new accounting standards to have been agreed upon and imposed on all companies in the world. Time is running out for inaction. I have a few suggestions. First, radical transparency. Life cycle analysis (LCA) has been defined as 'a method used to evaluate the environmental impact of a product through its life cycle, encompassing extraction and processing of the raw materials, manufacturing, distribution, use, recycling and final disposal'.[11] Using this as a template, we need LCAs to be available online for all agri-food ingredients so end products will be able to have a clear and informative electronic label readable by consumers, which will be assembled from all the LCAs of its ingredients. In turn the consumers will be able to make an informed choice, meaning our veggie-burger customer would have been able to see that their purchase ultimately has as disastrous a toll on the environment as a mass-produced meat patty.

Of course, LCAs shouldn't just become standard practice for the agri-food industry, but in every other sector, too, including consumer products and all industrial and construction projects (concrete, plastics, petrochemicals and so on). Recent deep tech and AI-based developments have made this technologically feasible today, but governments and large corporations still need a firm nudge from regulators – what's banned in the US and EU should be outlawed in South America, too – as well as from consumers (which, as I described in the Introduction, we are already seeing).

This means looking at how a business operates, and how it is valued, in a new, clear-eyed way (with rules and standards that in substance have yet to be written). As the *Financial Times*'s Alan Livsey wrote of another industry, steel: 'If a company was likely to face a bill in the future to buy permits to emit carbon, that is an impact that could be accounted for. Likewise, if an ageing steel plant had to be written down in value because its longevity is curtailed by tougher environmental standards, then an impairment is required.

'But how and which costs should be accounted are still being defined. I asked one steel sector analyst recently what they did to assess the financial impact of climate change on forecasts for the companies he covered. The response? Nothing. It was seen as too hard and there is too little clarity on what the standards of reporting should be.'[12]

(ii) A Multidimensional Approach

Second, I'm also advocating a proactive, multidimensional approach from investors (including fund managers), which means not only taking the full financial, economic, environmental and social cost of, say, soybean production in Brazil into account, but also measuring progress over time. My own impact investing firm, Astanor, for example, applies the venture capital philosophy to the creation of impact, with the aim of maximizing not only return, but impact. To do this we have defined a set of six impact KPIs (key performance indicators) that enable us to capture a holistic image of our companies' positive impacts on both people and the planet, across the entire agri-food value chain:

Planet: Three planet KPIs to efficiently assess how to address the challenge of climate change: GHG Emissions, Water Use & Biodiversity

People: Two people KPIs to measure our contribution to improving social and health crises: Social & Health

Enablers: A third category of KPIs, necessary to assure our collective advancement towards global climate goals. Today, we have one enabler KPI: Climate Tech Data

Throughout the book I'll be weaving in a handful of examples from the Astanor portfolio to illustrate how we measure for impact. The first of these is New York-based Modern Meadow, a next-generation materials company, which has developed what it terms 'bio alloy' technology, where plant-derived structural proteins are alloyed – or combined – with bio-based polymers to create a superior animal-free material that, for example, matches or exceeds traditional leather in functionality and aesthetic standards but also produces animal-free collagen for pharmaceutical and cosmetics applications. (As we'll see in Chapter 4, this plant-derived collagen alternative is not only cheaper than animal-derived collagen, but it can scale to very large volumes ultimately to end the need for the cosmetics and healthcare industries to raise and slaughter animals to procure collagen.) As a result, the start-up scores highly against three of our Impact Principles, which are relevant to them:

Regenerative: 3/5 – they use 100 per cent non-GMO (genetically modified organisms), organic soy; they favour co-products or second-generation crops. (Also, as it's derived directly from the crop, in this case soya, which is normally eaten by the cow and then transformed into collagen or skin, the process bypasses methane and CO_2 production, which therefore has an additional beneficial impact.)

Food integrity: 3/5 – certificate of origin and engagement with the soy protein and bio-based polyurethanes (bioPUs) suppliers; they act as a catalyst to raise the sustainability and accountability in adjacent industries.

Conserve: 5/5 – this is core to Modern Meadow's mission. It is founded on circularity, and responsible end-of-life principles; it results in a low-waste process.

From the company's vantage point, meanwhile, Andras Forgacs, Modern Meadow's co-founder and former CEO, explains that their own approach to measuring their sustainability is underpinned by three pillars. 'The first is the resources and inputs that are required to make our materials. For us, an important principle is being animal-free. Another important principle is that we feel an urgency to climate action. We're very mindful of our CO_2 and methane footprint, and of our interaction with livestock. So we want to circumvent that.

'The next pillar for us is about ecosystem impact. It's all well and good to go from livestock to plants, but you don't want to use a lot of land, you don't want to use a lot of water, and you don't want to exacerbate agricultural run-off, and eutrophication.

'And then the third pillar for us is end-of-use and circularity. We design our materials with end-of-use and circularity principles in mind. That third pillar is the hardest, because there are inherent tensions. The more durable you make materials, which certain applications require, which consumers value, especially for durable goods, the less easily it will biodegrade. Everything that goes into our materials is bio-based, and our technology has the potential to be biodegradable, but it's not a property we're optimizing above all others. So that's the tricky bit, the end of life. But in terms of carbon and ecosystem impact, I think we're doing quite well.'

When it comes to measuring it all, Modern Meadow use life cycle assessments* led by their head of sustainability. 'We look at both the direct impacts and the consequential impacts,' says Forgacs. 'From a direct impact standpoint we do well, but when you look at the consequences of our technologies, they are actually even better because we amplify the emergence of a bio-economy, even though that isn't initially reflected in an LCA.

---

* Author's note: the terms life cycle assessment and life cycle analysis are interchangeable.

'Life cycle assessments tend to be backward-looking; they are your rear-view mirror for technologies that you've already developed where you can make certain engineering assumptions about the operations at scale based on things that you've demonstrated. But you have to have a product and a process that's well developed.

'LCAs are not good for informing research and development that is forward-looking, which is why we use decision-based criteria. We've established a hierarchy of inputs, so that when our scientists at the bench need to make a decision, they have heuristics they can use that can allow them to make certain choices *a priori*.'

From the impact investor's side of the table, having a framework enables Astanor to track a company's performance against our KPIs, with the objective of improving their score against each indicator over time. We also measure each investment for alignment with relevant UN Sustainable Development Goals,[13] as well as with the EU Green Deal[14] – Modern Meadow, for example, was considered to be aligned with SDG 13 (Climate Action) due to its 'principle (of having) products and processes, first and foremost, with low greenhouse gas emissions and low depletion of fossil fuel resources'.

Measurement is therefore fundamental to the impact revolution and is why we should be incentivizing impact investor-backed start-ups that can be designed and built to measure the effect they have on people and the planet from day one. The fact that most of these companies are still privately held and backed by venture capital and private equity investors – driven by impact missions – makes them capable of resisting the assault of the die-hard Friedman doctrine investors that are so active on the public markets. As we'll see in Chapter 4, a large number of private companies in the climate-tech sector, for instance, have already in the space of just a few years begun to remedy longstanding problems.

(iii) Nature's Balance Sheet and the Cost of Repair

The multidimensional approach to investing I described exposes the deep flaws inherent in an accounting model that is no longer fit for purpose given the crisis in which we find ourselves. As outlined above, we must replace it with a new standard – the double or triple bottom line – which factors in the full financial, economic, environmental and social impact a company and its products or services have on the world. However, even that model would only make sense on its own if the planet was on a sustainable trajectory, and we were more or less replenishing the resources we extract or deplete. Instead, our impact on the world continues to be net negative, and we are therefore largely living on borrowed time. So, while having all the available data at our fingertips to inform better decision-making is critical, it's certainly not enough on its own. That's why we must also factor in *the cost of repair*.

If we look at the issue in legacy accounting terms, it's as if we are still fixated with nature's P&L account when we should also be considering its balance sheet (i.e. the complete picture of the planet on a given date, including all assets and liabilities). That latter 'scorecard' would encompass everything from the quality of the air we breathe, to that of the land, oceans and freshwater bodies, and the biodiversity teeming within it all.

Zeroing in on nature's balance sheet forces us to confront the complete picture and either replenish and remediate where we can – if it is feasible from a technological and financial standpoint to do so – or cease altogether activities that cannot be reversed. To succeed, clearly this would entail monitoring and holding to account those who fail to act within recognized guidelines, with the cost of replenishment being borne by the government department, company or organization responsible.

Monitoring and enforcement would be no small task. Yet there are promising signs that things are already beginning to move in the right direction at least in the crucial world of finance and investing. While at the helm at Danone, Emmanuel Faber, who started as CFO before turning into a sustainability-pioneer CEO, introduced carbon-adjusted EPS (earnings per share) reporting. He did this in part to spark a conversation with the food giant's shareholders; if they were going to be paid dividends in excess of the carbon-adjusted EPS amount (which would clearly be lower), that would de facto mean that Danone was failing to invest sufficiently for the future in reducing emissions, and in soil health to build a resilient regenerative agriculture business model, which would in turn affect long-term dividend payments. Faber's actions attracted widespread shareholder support as well as rating agencies support, resulting in a lower cost of borrowing for Danone.

'Now everyone is moving in the direction of more carbon disclosures for a number of reasons,' he says. 'First, governments are committed on pathways to carbon reduction through Nationally Determined Contributions (NDCs). And as we've seen in Europe – in Germany, in France and in the Netherlands – governments can be taken to court if they don't take the appropriate steps and miss targets; and companies may be as well.

'So there is now significant pressure on governments to act. And they will turn to business to deliver on decarbonization. Central banks have taken climate risk as part of their financial stability mandate, and they will also turn to banks and assets owners to decarbonize.

'Second, we're already seeing pressure from the customers of the large investment firms, which influence the latter's behaviour on climate issues.' He cites the example of global mining conglomerate Anglo American, which spun off its thermal coal-mining subsidiary, Thungela, in June 2021. Shares in the spin-off plunged by nearly a quarter on the first day of trading.[15] At the time this was viewed as symptomatic of investors' waning appetite for coal-mining stocks in the context of the climate crisis and government pledges to phase out coal. (However, the share price later rebounded as demand for coal soared amid the global energy crunch.)

But that's not all, says Faber. 'The EBITDA (earnings before interest, taxes, depreciation and amortization) multiple that they got at IPO was a third of (Thungela's) annual EBITDA. Normally that number would be maybe five or ten times an annual EBITDA. This is what's happening now when (both institutional and private) investors look at coal. Not only because they've made the calculation that the net present value might be about to go down quickly, largely because of unpredictable political or regulatory decisions about coal in the future, but also because nobody wants to touch that stock – they can't afford to be seen by NGOs (non-governmental organizations) and campaigning groups who would then talk to their customers such as the Harvard Foundation, the California State Teachers Retirement System (CalSTRS), the Japanese Government Pension Investment Fund and so on, and say, "You should blacklist these (fund managers) because they've invested in a pure coal mining venture." So, already, the cost of capital of these operations is being hurt, and the volatility in share price reflects the uncertainty of the future.'

There have also been a few funds, including leading US fund AQR Capital Management, who are pushing to obtain the right to decarbonize their portfolios, where they hold stocks in fossil fuel companies, through shorting that stock as a sort of carbon offset, Faber continues. 'Now you can imagine the effect that that will have on the share price of these companies if shorting is used as a strategy to decarbonize portfolios. That's not to say that a structural short selling strategy would be feasible at scale, but the company or industry-specific risk of short selling would pressurize the share price in these companies, which again would add to the cost of capital. So they are really feeling the heat as we speak.'

These developments are indicative of the sea change that's underway, Faber maintains. 'I can tell you that when stock exchanges, the IFRS, the Central Banks – including the European Central Bank – say that climate risk is part of their mandate, it really means that there is now clear alignment that the impact of global warming needs to be measured, and rewarded (or punished) by the capital markets so that finance can be in sync with the need for businesses to invest for the longer term.'

With all this in mind, let's return for a final time to our customer purchasing a 'guilt-free' veggie burger made from imported Brazilian soya. Note that we picked on soya burgers, but the environmental costs of plant-based burgers made of other plants such as pea proteins are not much better than non-regeneratively grown soya, with peas grown in intensive farms in Canada and shipped to China for processing into protein powder, without necessarily all the quality standards respected, and forwarded to Germany or the Netherlands to be manufactured into the burgers together with dubious flavourings and bindings for final distribution in the UK supermarkets.

Opting to phase out red-meat consumption in Europe and replace it with soybean burgers to boost sustainability currently ends with many (often) impoverished Brazilians facing deforestation, poisoned soil and water and infant deaths. If the full cost *including the cost of repair* is taken into account, the obvious conclusion in any rigorous LCA is that the ultimate cost of intensive soybean production in Brazil cannot be justified, and companies and government agencies should face prohibitive fines to force them to act more responsibly and repair the damage done, wherever possible.

Yet, as we'll see in Chapter 3, the modernization of our accounting model and incorporating the cost of repair into businesses' bottom lines, though absolutely critical, is only part of the overall solution. Philanthropists and foundations, who wield so much influence in this sphere, must also learn and apply the lessons of impact investing and mission alignment.

The outdated foundation model

Beyond philanthropy

Sometimes the pivotal moments in our lives come down to pure serendipity. One such moment came about when my future fellow impact investor Karl 'Charly' Kleissner and I happened to be looking for a new professional challenge at roughly the same time. It was late 2002, and I'd just left Benchmark Capital, after almost four years as a venture capitalist, following a decade as a software entrepreneur in Silicon Valley. Charly, meanwhile, had recently left Ariba, a software firm where he had been the first VP of engineering. Ariba had pioneered the field of online procurement automation and completed a successful IPO (initial public offering) in 1999, making the company one of the B2B icons of the 'dot.com boom'.

We met for coffee one December morning at a café in Los Gatos, a smallish town in the Bay Area, close to the Santa Cruz Mountains, best known today as the location of Netflix's headquarters, to hash out our future. Charly, who lived in Los Gatos for twenty years, says that he was 'in a state of flux' at the time. 'I'd stepped off the treadmill in the fall of 2001 and it had taken me about half a year to decompress,' he now recalls. 'After ten very intense years, my wife Lisa and I were starting to reimagine our lives.'

Right away Charly and I agreed on one thing: we'd both reached a point in our careers where we'd achieved financial security and wanted to do something more meaningful than selling yet more software to the world. Over successive coffees and teas, our conversation moved on to social entrepreneurship, an area of growing interest to us both. Lisa, an early Apple employee, had recently set up a foundation, KL Felicitas, where she was later joined by Charly, to channel a large part of their recently acquired wealth to non-profit projects. My thinking was also moving in this direction. I'd become increasingly convinced that I could use my experience as an entrepreneur and investor in the Valley to help companies with a social purpose have a positive impact on their surroundings and the wider world, by scaling up via the use of technology and management processes that had yet to permeate that particular field.

Charly and I went back a long way. He'd come to Silicon Valley from Vienna in 1987, while I had arrived from France in 1981, and our paths first collided when he joined NeXT Computer, Steve Jobs's second company, as director of engineering in the early 1990s. With multiple friends in common also working at NeXT, or still at Apple, it wasn't long before Charly and I encountered one another socially. As European engineer immigrants on the West Coast, who shared a passion for alpine skiing and burgundy-style wine – Austria and France have at least these two traits in common! – unsurprisingly we quickly established a rapport.

My own offices at RightPoint Software (previously known as DataMind), the data-mining software company that I had co-founded in 1993 and where I was president and CEO, were near NeXT's base on Seaport Boulevard in Redwood City. An outstanding engineering manager, Charly was working on the architecture for a new multimedia operating system. But NeXT wasn't doing particularly well at that time, in 1995, and as we needed to scale up our own engineering capacity at Rightpoint – having recently closed a funding round led by Sequoia Capital – I offered him a job as my right-hand man in charge of engineering and product. Intrigued by the pioneering way we were using Bayesian networks to build predictive models in the then nascent field of data-mining – and because the company was still in R&D mode, and therefore presented a stimulating challenge – he decided to jump ship and join me, a courageous decision when one knows Steve Jobs's character ...

As he joined Rightpoint, Charly brilliantly helped scale our company from R&D stage to enterprise-ready. However, two years later, as I repositioned RightPoint as a vertical application company ahead of an exit, I hired Earl Stahl, an experienced product and engineering manager, to help us with the transition, while Charly left us for Ariba, lured by their vision of automating, end-to-end, the procurement process for businesses, from ordering pencils to generating complex RFPs (requests for proposal).

But serendipity would soon bring us together again. A couple of years after that, I co-founded, in parallel, a separate company called Trading Dynamics with Dr Yoav Shoham, a Stanford University professor who had been working on applying game theory to the optimization of electronic marketplaces. Within a few weeks, I designed Trading Dynamics' main product: an online software toolbox that enabled the automatic generation of complex RFPs. It turned out that it was something that quickly became of strategic interest to Ariba. Ultimately, in 1999, my close relationship with Charly led to the acquisition of Trading Dynamics by Ariba, despite the best efforts of Ariba's main competitor, Commerce One, who pulled out all the stops to do the deal themselves.

A broken system

So it was against a backdrop of our frequently intersecting lives and careers that Charly and I came to be mulling over our futures that morning in 2002, in Los Gatos. As Lisa and Charly's foundation was already up and running, I wanted to hear about what they had learned from their experience thus far. Reflecting on their journey to date, Charly says their initial focus had been to support social entrepreneurship because that was a new concept back then and it was a viable alternative to both straightforward philanthropy – i.e. passive grant-giving – and pure capitalism, which he and Lisa consider to be fundamentally flawed. It was also a way of getting their hands dirty while helping social businesses adopt the best elements of technology start-ups – an approach I wholeheartedly endorsed.

As part of my own initial due diligence in the social entrepreneurship space, I went with Charly for a meeting at Rockefeller Philanthropy Advisors (RPA) in New York City to find out more about the traditional approach to philanthropy. Charly was working with then RPA vice-president Doug Bauer at the time, as he and Lisa immersed themselves in the workings of the philanthropic world. As outsiders from the Valley, it was obvious to us from the start that this tried and tested model for funding worthy causes was broken and, even worse, was specifically failing the poorest, and indeed the planet itself.

'When we looked into it, we saw that the classical way of (doing) philanthropy was actually as bad as the classical way of investing in the sense that it augmented systemic problems,' Charly says today. 'I wish Steve Jobs was around to challenge the old way of doing things. He wouldn't go along with the old philanthropic model, which only creates more dependencies and corruption.' He goes on to cite the example of the 2004 Indian Ocean earthquake and tsunami. 'The aid rarely gets to the people who need it. We saw it first hand in Sri Lanka after the tsunami. Billions of good dollars were spent but nothing came to the fishing villages we worked at (with Social Impact International).

'And yet these folks (from NGOs and charities) drove around in big Toyota Land Cruisers, checking everything out while very little changed (on the ground). So that's a clearly broken system,' he says, a trace of exasperation in his voice.

In fact, the underlying principles of philanthropy have scarcely changed since the industrial revolution: namely, that as a business founder, you build your empire without any regard for its impact on the world or your local community. Only once your fortune is made does your mind turn towards leaving a legacy and 'giving something back' by setting up a charitable foundation. This usually entails ploughing the foundation's capital into traditional investment vehicles to ensure the highest possible financial returns, while withdrawing about 5 per cent of the foundation's assets each year in the form of grants with which to operate charitable endeavours.[1]

The more enlightened foundations try to make longer-term commitments to particular NGOs, but by and large the model is you optimize your returns whatever it takes, and make small payouts to the cause or causes you support – even if this tried and tested method results in the ludicrous situation of, say, investing in companies that are detrimental to the environment, while simultaneously channelling a portion of your returns to an NGO that's set up to improve the very same environment you are helping to degrade. (There's even a case of a foundation dedicated to social justice investing in a mutual fund that, in turn, invests in private correctional facilities.)

There were around $1 trillion in endowments of grant-making foundations in the US in 2017, the most recent year for which data is publicly available.[2] Charly estimates that, at most, 3 per cent of that capital is aligned with the mission of these grant-making bodies, which leaves approximately $970 billion invested in non-mission-aligned positions that are not just nullifying the good deeds being carried out by the grant's activities of these foundations, but in some cases actively undermining them.

This entire system is thus skewed towards entrenching the status quo and has a net negative impact on the wider world. Looking at the problem with fresh eyes, as entrepreneurs tend to, it was plain to us back then that all investments made by foundations should be entirely aligned with the organization's overall mission. Yet this was considered – at that time – a shockingly radical approach.

Over the years since, synching missions and portfolios in this way came to be known as mission-aligned investing.[3] Immediately twenty times more powerful, an example of this approach is the Mary Reynolds Babcock Foundation,[4] which is focused on combatting poverty in the Southern US.[5] That mission explicitly underscores all 'the organization's investment decisions regarding its endowment, encompassing program-related investments, community development, financial institutions, and market-rate investments that pass environmental, social and governance scrutiny'.

Making an impact

This mission-aligned approach led, in turn, to the concept of impact investing, which at a high level is about aligning the goals much earlier on in the process, and investing up to 100 per cent of a foundation's (or more commonly these days, of a dedicated impact fund's) capital in projects aligned with its purpose – and then, crucially, measuring that impact against certain yardsticks. Charly, an early practitioner, defines it as follows: 'For me impact investing means that positive – and negative, for that matter – impact is explicitly integrated into every decision-making process within an investment, be that planning, the transaction itself, reporting, or figuring out how the impact actually worked out and improving on that. This is as opposed to being an add-on like CSR (corporate social responsibility) or ESG, where they add on impact after the fact.'

I quickly became infected by Charly's enthusiasm for impact investing, even if I continue to believe that ESG, if used correctly and honestly, can already make a big difference to outcomes.

Yet there is an inherent superiority to impact investing. Everything else runs the risk of becoming impact-washing (which is where a start-up or a fund makes exaggerated or false claims about their beneficial impact on people or the planet.)

The modern roots of impact investing most likely lie in socially responsible investing (SRI) borne out of social and civil rights movements in the 1960s, which led to heightened awareness of issues of responsibility and accountability.[6] An example is anti-war protestors demanding that university endowments no longer invest in defence contractors. 'Impact investors believe that by investing in business models that address social and environmental challenges, such as the diabetes epidemic or climate change, they can generate market-rate financial returns while also delivering measurable impact on the targeted problem,' wrote Brian Trelstad in 'Impact Investing: A Brief History'.[7]

Over time many noted philanthropists came to the same conclusion, namely that the old model needed to be radically overhauled. Laurene Powell Jobs (Steve's widow) launched Emerson Collective, a social change organization that uses impact investing in scalable for-profit, mission-aligned enterprises as an important part of its investment strategy. (Only a portion of her efforts go into direct grant-making for some very specific non-profits.) Similarly, eBay founder and chairman Pierre Omidyar and his wife Pamela transformed their foundation in 2004 into a for-profit, impact investing organization, Omidyar Network.

Meanwhile it was Pierre Omidyar – whom I'd got to know at Benchmark Capital, who funded eBay at the start of its journey, and with whom I worked closely on the launch of Benchmark Capital Europe in 2000–01 – who first introduced me to Ashoka.[8] Founded some twenty years earlier by management consultant-turned-'godfather of social entrepreneurship' Bill Drayton, Ashoka was established to find and support the world's most ambitious social entrepreneurs. Omidyar had invested $5 million into Ashoka's launch into Europe, and I became involved in 2002, for a couple of years, among other things to help create the Ashoka Support Network and assist in the hiring of former French Olympic wrestler-turned-social entrepreneur Arnaud Mourot to launch Ashoka in France, Belgium and Switzerland.

However, while it had certainly developed a finely tuned and effective system for identifying great social entrepreneurs, Ashoka, at that time, was primarily focused on producing reports (alongside offering small one-off financial stipends), rather than providing the necessary long-term financial support and hands-on guidance to social entrepreneurs 'on the ground'. Since offering practical advice based on my experience was the main thing I brought to the table, my search for the right vehicle with which to make the maximum impact would have to continue.

Beyond philanthropy

In 2004, a couple of years after our coffee in Los Gatos, and after evaluating multiple ideas, Charly proposed that we start an impact accelerator together in India. This was not yet a fully fledged plan but built on our many discussions with other foundations and social entrepreneur backers over the previous eighteen months. As he said it back then, three planks would underpin our project. First, it would be about on-the-ground, peer-to-peer learning between the social entrepreneurs and the Valley contingent. Second, the founders would have access to a meaningful amount of capital. Third, there would be a focus on capacity building, essentially around helping founders to scale.

Initially Charly had envisioned that we would do the project in partnership with a European or North American university. But a marketing study we commissioned from Kim Alter, a very experienced practitioner, convinced us otherwise when it reported back saying that while the model and the three planks were highly innovative, the accelerator should be launched in Africa or India, rather than Europe or the US, where it would have far more impact.

And so, it was in 2005 that Charly and I – joined in this family-led philanthropic project by our wives Lisa Kleissner and Sophie Archambeau – travelled to India to set up Social Impact International. We were joined the following year by a friend of mine in London, Peter Wheeler, a recently retired banker from Goldman Sachs who wanted to move into social entrepreneurship. So began a fascinating yet at times somewhat frustrating journey that would take us not only to India, but to Central America, Hawaii and Eastern Europe, where we road-tested a more pared-back model of impact investing, by directly supporting non-profits established to solve important social and environmental problems in real-world situations.

In India, which we visited many times over an intense five-year period, for example, we supported irrigation systems to allow farmers to become more efficient, a multi-village dried mango commercial project that had to overcome quality-control issues, and an ambitious banana peel recycling enterprise (a bigger problem than it sounds!).

While the venture was in many ways highly innovative for its time – for example, we made a conscious decision to have a 50:50 male to female ratio among participants – some elements didn't live up to our hopes. The entrepreneurs we funded invariably lacked the know-how, financial or managerial, to scale their ideas; indeed, many were resistant to the VC notion of scaling up altogether. Ultimately, however, we learned a great deal and turned the problem around by merging the best of these two worlds: the purpose-driven *raison d'être* of non-profits with the power and discipline of profit-seeking companies. That effective hybrid model of proto-impact investing enabled us to attract investors who were drawn by the possibility of meaningful financial returns after a given period, as opposed to simply writing endless checks to charities. Money began to flow into these organizations.

Meanwhile, my own personal journey from start-ups to the world of non-profits – alongside my spell at INSEAD and, as I rejoined Wellington Partners in London as a managing partner, venture investing in start-ups like Spotify, Betfair and XING – finally led me to take the logical next step towards fully fledged impact investing. In 2010 I co-founded Quadia Impact Finance, one of the first impact investing firms to go beyond philanthropy to build a portfolio where there is complete alignment between our vision of more a sustainable world and all our investable assets.

Once again serendipity played its part. Guillaume Taylor, a private banker I knew in Geneva – who had started his career at Intel Capital, working for my long-time business partner George Coelho – told me he'd been keenly following our activities at Social Impact International, and was eager to get involved in the space. What's more, he could bring a couple of deep-pocketed clients, who were similarly interested in the impact investing world, along with him, he said. We agreed that if and when he left his current role to set up a new impact fund, I would become an investor. That ended up happening rather sooner than anticipated, when I decided to help Guillaume start Quadia, his new impact investing entity, not just as a client and first investor, but as chairman of its board. And as we began to develop a portfolio of impactful start-ups in various domains ranging from micro-finance loans to soil remediation and reforestation projects, I became progressively more interested in the sustainable food and agri-tech space – areas which would go on to become the defining focus of the rest of my career.

Two decades have passed since my convivial morning with Charly in Los Gatos – and although we took somewhat separate and circuitous routes to get there, we arrived at strikingly similar conclusions. First that the traditional philanthropy model – of investing accumulated wealth to achieve maximum yield, to put just 5 per cent of it to work towards a positive impact on society and the planet – was not just broken, it had become a major part of the problem. So there needed to be alignment between the mission and all the investments a foundation makes.

But that on its own doesn't go anywhere near far enough.

Second, that while social entrepreneurship is an important stepping stone and plenty of great work is done by founders in the field, ultimately nibbling away on the periphery between businesses and non-profits/NGOs, both of which feed the status quo, is 'an exercise in futility' (as Charly puts it). Social entrepreneurs on their own cannot change the system. If you want to have an impact on the towering issues of our time – climate change, inequality and social justice, and poverty – then the design flaws of the economic system itself must be addressed. And the only way to achieve that is through impact, measurement and iteration.

Finally, from an entrepreneur's standpoint, instead of creating a company that has no positive impact on – or actively harms – the wider world, founders need to focus on building companies, of equal value, that as a matter of course are impactful from day one. That way there's a continuum from the very beginning of an entrepreneur's career to their retirement, where they are always having a positive impact on the goals they've set themselves, not just in the twilight of their working lives, but for the entirety of their journey.

Impact investing in climate tech

Vanishing packaging and plastic-eating bacteria

Let's not pull our punches. To place humanity and our interactions with Earth back on a sustainable trajectory and stand any chance of slowing climate change in its tracks, we must drastically reduce, and then cease altogether, the release of any additional greenhouse gases into the atmosphere. As Bill Gates argues in *How to Avoid a Climate Disaster*, the sheer scale of this challenge is momentous: 'The world has never done anything quite this big,' he writes. 'Every country will need to change its ways.'[1] In fact it will require nothing short of a revolution in almost every aspect of our daily lives, from heating our homes to producing food to moving about. Crucially, this 'revolution' won't be achieved simply by demanding that people radically cut down on their consumption of goods and services. Coercion will play a role, but only at the margins. Rather, success requires disruptive new technologies to equip us with sustainable and regenerative ways to do the things we do today, but to do so without forcing us to change our habits or reduce our quality of life.

Only new technology can smooth our transition to this new era, and alongside the big nation-state levers we can pull, including most obviously slashing emissions through the phasing out of fossil fuels, and the radical overhaul of our approach to finance as described in Chapter 2, it is one of the most powerful, and as yet little utilized, weapons in our arsenal with which to achieve net zero. This cluster of exciting new technologies, overwhelmingly delivered by impact-backed start-ups, has collectively come to be known as climate tech.

First, what do we mean by that catch-all term? In the comprehensive *The State of Climate Tech 2020*, which was updated the following year, services giant PwC defines this cluster of innovations as 'technologies that are explicitly focused on reducing GHG emissions or addressing the impact of global warming...'[2] The term, they continue, is 'purposefully broad in order to incorporate the broad swathe of technologies and innovations being used to address GHG emissions and the broad array of industries where they are being applied'. Five key sectors are then identified: energy; mobility and transport; food, agriculture and land use; heavy industry; the built environment and construction. To these I would add a number of sub-categories including consumer goods, fast fashion and e-commerce.

Yet, as we've seen in Chapter 1, some of these categories are far more significant sources of GHG emissions than others – as illustrated by a unique piece of research published in *Nature Climate Change* in May 2020 during the first COVID-19 lockdown.[3] Even though an estimated 3.9 billion people in ninety countries – roughly half of the world's population[4] – went into lockdown, borders were closed, and much of the rich world stopped travelling, commuting, eating out, shopping in brick-and-mortar stores, going to school and so on, daily global CO_2 emissions had decreased by *just 17 per cent* by early April compared with the mean 2019 levels.

And despite that fall, the following month, in May 2020, the concentration of carbon dioxide in the atmosphere was the highest ever recorded in human history at about 418 parts per million, according to a *National Geographic* report on the research.[5] How so?

'Over 80% of the water is still gushing into the tub'

The answer lies in the fact that a fleeting drop like this registers as barely a blip in the overall levels of CO_2 already released into the atmosphere. The *Nat Geo* report likened Earth's atmosphere to a bathtub, with human-driven emissions in this scenario the water surging out of the tap. 'When a momentous event like this pandemic happens to push CO_2 emissions down, it's as if the bath's tap has been shut down by 17%' declares the article's author Alejandra Borunda. 'But over 80% of the water is still gushing into the tub, so the water level in the tub will still rise.'

The 17 per cent figure is significant in another way, too. Given that much of humanity were confined to their homes – and that emissions dropped by less than a fifth – then it once again crystallizes how the transport and logistics sector generally would scarcely alter the velocity of the climate crisis even if it ceased altogether. And yet this is the very sector that has been the focus of arguably more attention than any other in recent years from environmental campaigners, pundits and policymakers.

There is, it seems, much mileage (not to mention tax revenue) to be squeezed from singling out the use of fossil-fuel-powered cars, ships and planes, despite the fact that the entire sector represents just 16 per cent of the total GHG emissions pie, with domestic and international aviation (passenger and freight) around 2 per cent of that figure.[6] During lockdown, the climate crisis grew more serious still precisely because everything else – from our overall extractive exploitation of the land and oceans to the energy-devouring internet economy – was still humming away as loudly as ever.

Towards energy independence

The race between climate change and energy independence (where we are no longer dependent upon carbon), once considered all but unwinnable, is almost won at least from a technological standpoint. This was made possible in large part thanks to a group of visionary impact investors who grasped the urgency of switching to renewable energy sources – and all that would involve from a developmental and manufacturing standpoint – as far back as the early 2000s.

The traditional energy giants (oil and gas companies, as well as energy utilities) had a vested interest in optimizing the use of fossil fuels (alongside some nuclear) for the next century, the corollary of which was a failure to invest meaningfully in R&D of renewable sources. Indeed, they had little incentive to do so, not least because the legacy accounting system does not factor in externalities including CO_2 emissions or other side effects such as biodiversity loss caused by extracting and burning fossil fuels (see Chapter 2). What's more, the global financial system rewards incumbent players – especially the largest of them – anyway.

Without the sheer dogged determination of these aforementioned impact investors, and their conviction to swim against the tide (supported in the public sphere by a few outliers like Al Gore), we certainly would not have been in the position that we find ourselves today, where approaching a third of global electricity generation comes from renewable sources[7] – indeed, in the UK that figure stood at 41.6 per cent in the first quarter of 2021[8] – and renewables are well on their way to meeting the overwhelming majority of humanity's energy needs within the foreseeable future. That would have been almost unimaginable just twenty-five years ago.

But let's step back a moment and remind ourselves how we got here. Until the nineteenth and early twentieth centuries, energy production was essentially decentralized (see Chapter 1). 'Older civilizations … used flowing water, wind, and animals to perform work and move people and goods,' writes Michael E. Weber in his book *Power Trip: The Story of Energy*. 'The classic European image of a windmill or medieval water wheel that powered a mill to grind grain, saw wood, or polish glass is a cliché indicating an older society.'

Fast-forward to the end of the nineteenth century and the arrival of the incandescent light bulb, when the first known wind turbine was built in Scotland in 1887 by Professor James Blyth of Anderson's College, Glasgow (today Strathclyde University), who used the resulting power to light his holiday cottage – a world first – according to a brief history of wind turbines published by Renewable Energy World.[9] (Incidentally, Blyth offered to supply the surplus energy produced by his turbine to the local high street, but was reportedly turned down by locals who considered electricity 'the work of the devil'.) A year later, the first known US wind turbine was created for electricity production, built by inventor Charles Brush to provide power for his Ohio mansion, again illustrating the notion of hyper-localized energy production and supply.

However, around the same time an early version of centralized electricity began to take root. Weber writes that 'the world's first hydroelectric power plant was built in 1879 along the Fox River to light hundreds of bulbs in Appleton, Wisconsin. The first hydroelectric dams were not very large and were more reminiscent of the medieval overshot waterwheels used for mechanical power.' By the late 1800s, such smaller hydroelectric power plants had started to proliferate to meet the growing demand for light bulbs and small motors for industrial work, Weber continues. 'By the end of the 1880s, factories had begun to electrify. In 1900, only 4% of Chicago's factories were electrified; thirty years later, it was 78%.'

By the middle of the twentieth century electricity generation had become all about mass-scale centralized production in the form of (coal and natural gas-fired and nuclear) power plants. And with the system of power generation, transmission and distribution that sprung up so complex – in the US, for example, it is controlled by a patchwork of investor-owned, public and independent entities – and demand for oil[10] and natural gas[11] rising slowly yet inexorably, why would any of the largest players in the ecosystem want to upend a status quo that has served so many so well for so long?

Against this backdrop, where few were yet aware of the environmental fallout caused by fossil fuels, a first wave of investors (impact investors in all but name), scientists and entrepreneurs began to focus on renewables. In the early-to-mid-2000s, they funded R&D in solar cell (the electrical devices that convert light energy into electrical energy) technology, biomass transformation and wind power.

One of the prime movers in the space at the time were members of the Brenninkmeijer family – the German-Dutch dynasty whose forebears founded the textile-turned-clothing retailer C&A in 1841 in Sneek, Holland. Today C&A is part of COFRA,[12] a privately held group of companies based in Zug, Switzerland, spanning retail, real estate and investing, wholly owned by some fifty descendants of C&A's founders. In 2002, a key investment, through Good Energies – a subsidiary of COFRA focused on environmental technology – was made in German solar cell maker Q-Cells, which helped pave the way for future solar cell technology.[13]

While the company had little by way of truly proprietary technology back then (in fact they were using off-the-shelf equipment to produce standard multi-crystalline solar cells), Q-Cells' founders had understood before anyone else some important things about how the sector was poised to take off, recalls Christian Reitberger, an early investor into the company while a partner at Apax Partners in Munich.

'At the time of the investment, Germany had already introduced the feed-in tariff system (in the Renewable Energy Act of 2000) which meant that if you were a producer of renewable energy, the national grid had to buy the electricity that you generated and they had to pay you a fixed price per kilowatt hour for twenty years,' he says. 'And that price was very high initially.

'That gave certainty to buyers of solar modules, and of wind turbines, that they would be able to sell their renewable electricity for the next twenty years at a fixed price. It also gave total clarity – including planning clarity – on the revenue side to both individuals who put solar panels on their home roofs, and large solar or wind power plant operators. And that, in turn, caused the explosion of renewable energy deployment in Germany, and in the end led to the industrialization of this new technology.'

As part of his due diligence, Reitberger held a series of private meetings in Berlin with political leaders, who held the energy brief, and was assured that their commitment to the feed-in tariff was steadfast. Moreover, because there was broad consensus on the issue across the main parties, the policy would even survive a change in government. 'So, it was clear to me then that demand would explode,' he says.

'It was also clear to the leadership team of Q-Cells and the vital thing they did was secure supply of silicon wafers, which is the starter product for PV cells. And nobody else did that back then; (their rivals) all thought that as they were already growing at around 10 per cent a year, and that that steady growth would continue, they didn't need to pre-order anything or enter into long-term supply contracts with wafer manufacturers. But Q-Cells thought differently – and struck long-term supply agreements with many of the wafer manufacturers out there to lock in supply.'

The other crucial thing they did was start to build manufacturing facilities, otherwise known as Fabs, at scale. 'When we invested, they had just built their first Fab. It had already started to work and was generating maybe €10 million in revenues. So rather than any kind of genuine product innovation, this industrialization approach was Q-Cells' true innovation. And they very quickly became the market leader in the space, because no one else had secured supply, and no one else had realized the full implications of the feed-in tariff law, which initially generated a German market, but was then widely adopted across Europe and so became an export market.'

Then, over time, as Q-Cells became profitable and scaled, the company began to build out a large R&D engineering team to focus on product and process innovation, Reitberger says. 'But the most important thing to understand about Q-Cells is that they kicked off the industrialization of this technology and without them (driving down costs through achieving economies of scale) this industry wouldn't have ramped up (when it did).'

Around the same period, Valley-based VCs also channelled large sums into what was by then known as 'cleantech', encompassing solar, biofuels and hydrogen fuel cell technology. Investment surged in 2006, with cleantech start-ups garnering some $1.75 billion in VC funding. But as a paper from MIT ('Venture Capital and Cleantech: The Wrong Model for Clean Energy Innovation'[14]) concluded, five years later the entire sector was in a state of 'shambles' with high-profile casualties including cylindrical solar tubes manufacturer Solyndra, which had received $500 million in federal loan guarantees, but ended up filing for bankruptcy. Overall, between 2006 and 2011, VCs invested $25 billion into the cleantech sector and lost over half of it.

Q-Cells was another casualty of the era. The company filed for bankruptcy in 2011, before being snapped up by South Korean conglomerate Hanwha Group a year later. It had been a victim of the perfect storm that struck the renewable energy sector in the early 2010s. Energy being a commodity, the race to price-parity per kWh of electricity produced by solar cells versus per kWh produced by coal- or gas-fired plants was the most important metric that investors looked for. To achieve that, both solar cell technology and manufacturing had to evolve. As Christian Reitberger described, Q-Cells was an outlier in this regard, and the company was on a path to achieving price parity with traditional energy sources, when two things knocked it off course.

First was the development and exploitation of shale gas reserves achieved by another technological breakthrough – fracking (and AI-based exploration) – which reduced the cost of producing electricity from gas-powered plants considerably, thereby lengthening the path to price-parity per kWh for Q-Cells in a short period of time. Then the Chinese government – having determined renewables to be of key strategic interest to their future economy – awarded, via state-owned banks, zero-interest loans worth tens of billions of dollars to new companies formed to win the solar cell sector, thereby undercutting incumbent producers.

Alongside those developments, in the West and in Europe in particular, the financial crisis of 2008–09 and its long tail meant that the private banking sector had withdrawn support for the loss-making renewables sector; (it was lossmaking in large part because of the shale gas bonanza that they were all too happy to finance). This combination tipped Q-Cells, and other first-wave cleantech companies, over the edge.

Yet, significant progress had been forged, and as I've already argued, the investments made in early renewables played a very important part. Indeed, one can certainly make the case that even a trillion-dollar company like Tesla, founded in 2003, has emerged as the poster child for cleantech VC investments of that period in much the same way as Amazon emerged from the dot.com crash of 2000.

As for Q-Cells, Reitberger – although 'wary of self-glorification' – describes the venture money that was ploughed into the company as 'absolutely mission critical'. He recalls: 'I wasn't the first investor in this company. There was a visionary investor before us – Good Energies – who came in after a number of business angels had seed-funded the company. Without their initial money and without Apax growth money, six or nine months later, Q-Cells for sure would not have been able to ramp as quickly. It would still have been founded by a great group of visionaries – they did not need us for that – but the trajectory it took, which was not linear as it was for the rest of the industry, but really exponential – which is what was needed to get the cost curve down … I think venture capital was instrumental in that. And that rapid expansion, which lifted the whole market, was ignited by venture capital.'

Indeed, it is in large part due to the groundwork laid by these early impact investors that we are in a situation today where we have all the technology building blocks in place to do the things we must do – from agriculture and food to transportation, manufacturing and fast fashion – to create a world run on sustainable energy without compromising too drastically on our lifestyle. The problem is the absence of political will and the leadership necessary to accelerate the transition away from extractive energy sources.

And that is no mere sideshow. It is in fact absolutely at the heart of humanity's journey towards a zero-emissions economy. For example, while aviation and autos have been the subject of a barrage of carbon taxes and regulatory frameworks across the world in the quest to drive down GHG emissions – and innovation in the space is anyway nibbling away at the problem – the far more significant issue of the sidelining of civilian nuclear power, by some of the key developed economies, garners precious little attention.

'A profoundly manmade disaster'

Let's consider for a moment why this is. The Fukushima Daiichi nuclear disaster, in which three of the plant's six reactors melted down, was the worst nuclear accident since Chernobyl a quarter of a century earlier. Although an exhaustive Japanese parliamentary committee report – which included 900 hours of hearings and 1,100 interviews over a six-month period – concluded that the accident was 'a profoundly manmade disaster that could and should have been foreseen and prevented',[15] the perception that nuclear power is inherently risky was only reinforced. In Fukushima's aftermath, for example, Germany committed to the phasing out of nuclear power altogether. (As did, among others, Switzerland, Belgium and Spain.[16]) Yet as far back as 2006, Angela Merkel – a physicist before she became chancellor of Germany – had been an outspoken proponent of nuclear power, criticizing her predecessor Gerhard Schröder's government for opting to phase it out. 'I will always consider it absurd to shut down technologically safe nuclear power plants that don't emit CO_2,' Merkel said at the time.

The data would appear to support Merkel's cool-headed assessment. An average European town of 187,090 people consumes one terawatt-hour of electricity per year. If that town were to be powered entirely by coal, twenty-five people would die prematurely annually (mostly from air pollution). Powered exclusively by oil, eighteen inhabitants would die prematurely every year. If powered only by gas, fatalities would fall to three people. If nuclear was the sole energy source for the town, nobody would die regularly from it. Hannah Ritchie, co-author of Our World In Data, says of nuclear power, '(a) death rate of 0.07 per terawatt-hour means it would take 14 years before a single person would die … (and) this might even be an overestimate'.[17] In his book *Rationality: What It Is, Why It Seems Scarce, Why It Matters* (2021), Steven Pinker writes: 'Nuclear power is the safest form of energy humanity has ever used … Yet (it) has stalled for decades in the United States and is being pushed back in Europe, often replaced by dirty and dangerous coal.'[18]

Where, then, did this stigma surrounding nuclear originate?

Even though Chernobyl comes first to mind for most people, I believe the nuclear stigma originates from an irrational conflation of nuclear weapons and civilian nuclear power plants, which began to gain traction in post-war Germany. Despite becoming progressively dishonest – as evidence that nuclear is a safe way to generate electricity mounted[19] – this highly politicized idea, peddled by German ecologists and other campaigners, first came to a head when large numbers of protestors converged and marched in 1974 in the town of Wyhl, on the edge of the Black Forest, where a nuclear power plant had been planned.[20] The protest, which led to violent clashes between activists and the authorities, turned out to be a successful one for campaigners when plans for the nuclear power plant were shelved a year later. As noted by the media company Deutsche Welle, events in Wyhl led to a number of other protests in the late 1970s and spawned a grassroots anti-nuclear movement which 'brought together church organizations, farmers and concerned local residents – along with student activists, academics, and peace protestors who saw a link between nuclear power and the atom bomb'. This broad coalition would ultimately morph into the Green Party, which won its first seats in Germany's federal parliament in 1983 (and 118 seats in the 2021 general election[21]).

Viewed against that background, it is easy to see why Fukushima (with its echoes of Chernobyl) changed the political weather, in Germany at least. Three months after the calamity, the German parliament voted to phase out atomic energy by the end of 2022 and replace it with renewables.[22] That went the way of many government energy pledges. By 2020, renewables represented 44.6 per cent of Germany's energy sources, while nuclear was still at 11.4 per cent.[23]

In July 2020 Germany's parliament voted to phase out coal power by no later than 2038. Yet this 'landmark act' drew serious flak, according to Clean Energy Wire, 'for falling short of climate targets and granting coal companies too much (financial) compensation'.[24] Indeed, in that very same year, lignite (brown coal) still provided some 17 per cent of Germany's energy mix, while data compiled by Fraunhofer ISE revealed that electricity generated from lignite actually *increased* in Europe's largest economy by 35 per cent over the first quarter of 2021 compared with the same period in 2020.[25]

And Germany is far from alone in prolonging its reliance on coal: the world's two leading emitters, China and the US, who along with the EU and India are responsible for over half of all GHG emissions, were both projected[26] to see coal consumption rise in 2021,[27] as I write.

It's true that some positive news on the eventual 'phase down' of coal emerged from the UN COP26 in Glasgow, with countries agreeing to 'accelerate efforts towards' phasing down 'unabated coal power' – which, as the *Financial Times* points out, refers to power plants that do not use technology to capture their CO_2 emissions.[28] Yet as was widely reported at the time, at the eleventh hour India and China watered down the wording in the deal text on coal from 'phase out' to 'phase down', drawing a swift rebuke from, among others, Greenpeace International's executive director Jennifer Morgan who said: '(The agreement) is meek, it's weak and the 1.5C goal is only just alive, but a signal has been sent that the era of coal is ending. And that matters.'[29]

All of which brings us back to nuclear. Political caution over this endlessly controversial, but clean power source, along with the necessity of keeping the lights on, inevitably means a short-term acceleration in GHG emissions, while pushing the target of viably reaching net zero ever further out of reach.

Yet fortunately other leading nations are notably more sanguine about nuclear power than some of those I've mentioned, recognizing the important role it can play in the energy mix alongside renewables. France currently derives about 70 per cent of its energy needs from nuclear – and President Macron recently announced that the country will embark on an ambitious plan to build up to fourteen new nuclear reactors both to guarantee energy independence and help achieve carbon neutrality[30] – while in 2020, Canada's federal government committed to a road map to encourage the deployment of small modular reactors (SMRs)[31], which produce zero carbon emissions and can be mass-produced far more cost effectively and quickly than large-scale nuclear power plants.[32] 'We don't see a path where we reach net-zero carbon emissions by 2050 without nuclear,' Seamus O'Regan, Canada's natural resources minister, declared.[33]

In the UK, which generates about 21 per cent of its power from nuclear, it was recently confirmed that Rolls-Royce Holdings (as opposed to the auto maker) had been backed by a consortium of private investors, alongside the British government, to develop SMRs to generate cleaner energy.[34] Although limited in scope, this deal does suggest a long-overdue shift in approach.

Indeed Bill Gates – an investor, founder and chairman in nuclear start-up TerraPower,[35] and therefore with skin in the game – believes this type of decentralized nuclear will become politically acceptable again precisely because it's safer than oil, coal and natural gas. In *How to Avoid a Climate Disaster*, he writes of TerraPower: 'Because no one was going to let us build experimental reactors in the real world, we set up a lab of supercomputers in Bellevue, Washington, where the team runs digital simulations of different reactor designs ...

'TerraPower's reactor could run on many different types of fuel, including the waste from other nuclear facilities. The reactor would produce far less waste than today's plants, would be fully automated – eliminating the possibility of human error – and could be built underground, protecting it from attack ...'[36]

However, later in the book he concedes that despite nuclear being 'the only carbon-free energy source we can use almost anywhere, 24 hours a day, 7 days a week ...', and the fact that SMRs are cheaper, safer and produce much less waste, 'without the right policies and the right approach to markets, the scientific and engineering work on these advanced reactors will go nowhere'.[37] In other words, we're back to the perennial problem of lack of political will.

Meanwhile, although renewables are now increasingly cheaper than fossil-fuel-derived energy,[38] they are no panacea – yet. Due to unresolved issues such as night-time intermittency and seasonal variations, renewable energy alone (given that wind and solar are associated with costly batteries) falls far short of meeting real-world, especially peak, energy requirements. And that's before you get on to the outsized demands from large-scale industrial users.

Given all of the above, if we are indeed committed to reaching net-zero energy generation by 2050, it's difficult to escape the conclusion that it can only be achieved with nuclear energy plugging the gap. (Certainly the combination of the two – i.e. renewables and nuclear – can also help wean us off fossil fuels entirely. Only not yet.)

In September 2020 the Energy Transitions Commission, a coalition of global leaders from across the energy sector – with a self-confessed mission to define how to reach net zero while ensuring developing countries can attain the developed world's standards of living – issued its latest report, declaring that it is 'undoubtedly technically and economically possible to achieve net-zero GHG emissions by around mid-century'.[39] Yet the finite stock of extractive energy on our planet still threatens to derail our progress.

The fact remains that if we have not found a way to fully switch to renewable systems, without upping the role of nuclear, before that approaching cliff edge – including by generating the energy required for building the solar cells, windmill blades and so on to get us there – then the underpinning of everything from global trade to our lives at home will come grinding to a halt.

'Bacteria that eat faux-plastics'

Regulators and tax incentives have helped accelerate the ongoing – and critics might say somewhat stuttering – transition to energy independence. According to PwC, as of 2020 'the policy and regulatory environment is increasingly more supportive, with 120 national governments having made commitments to decarbonize their economies with commensurate spending and policy action across both regulatory standards, e.g. bans and phase-outs to market-based measures, including carbon pricing'.[40]

Impact investors have become integral to this shift, too, as evidenced by the way the global impact market grew from $502 billion in AUM (assets under management) in 2018[41] to $715 billion in 2020,[42] according to data gathered by the Global Impact Investment Network (GIIN). In their updated 'State of Climate Tech 2021' report,[43] PwC revealed that climate tech now accounts for 14 cents of every venture capital dollar invested. Moreover, the average deal size nearly quadrupled over the first half of 2021, on the preceding year, growing from $27 million to $96 million, with 'megadeals becoming increasingly common'.

With just ten years to slash global GHG emissions before the planet warms up by a fatidic 1.5°C, several forces are converging to funnel this increased investment into the climate tech space. These include: the use of new and cheaper technologies; ramped-up consumer demand; new commitments from city authorities and national governments alike, alongside businesses, investors and above all consumers (and voters) demanding a commitment to decarbonization, sustainable business practices and transparency when it comes to charting progress.[44]

While still at a relatively early stage, well-resourced start-ups embracing new and emerging technologies to build scalable companies are, alongside the decarbonizing efforts of governments and international bodies, the only realistic means by which to curb emissions permanently. And in sector after sector, they are beginning to make significant inroads. Here's a snapshot of a few standout examples:

(i) The Built Environment/Construction

As the developing world industrializes, demand for chemicals, concrete and metals is set only to intensify. Therefore energy-efficiency measures and even regulatory efforts to choke off demand will not be sufficient to send emissions into reverse. Cement and steel are the biggest culprits. For each ton of cement produced, around a ton of CO_2 is released from the chemical reaction that produces it. For steel, 1.8 tons of CO_2 are released for each ton of steel produced from iron in a furnace. For plastics (ethylene) the equivalent figure is 1.3 tons.[45] (And this does not include CO_2 emissions from electricity production.)

The problem is compounded by the fact that the volume of steel and concrete production globally is projected to keep growing, led by the planet's two most populous countries, China and India, who are still in the thick of rapid infrastructure development. On current trends, cautions Gates, the world will produce roughly 2.8 billion tons of steel every year by 2050, thus adding up to 5 billion tons of CO_2 annually by then. For cement, production might continue to be at roughly the current level of 4 billion tons annually, thereby releasing another 4 billion tons of CO_2 per year.

Buildings and construction (including the operational costs of heating, cooling and lighting buildings) are responsible for 39 per cent of global GHG emissions all told,[46] according to the World Green Building Council. Yet while the built environment is a major emitter, the sector itself is so vast, representing 13 per cent of global GDP, worth $9.5 trillion – and, relative to most sectors, slow to harness new technology – that it offers almost unlimited scope for innovation.

I sit on the advisory board of 2150.vc, a new fund which backs tech companies doing the hard yards in the development of sustainable cities.[47] One area of particular interest to the fund is what's sometimes known as 'carbon accounting', where – based on similar principles to impact investing – the full direct and indirect emissions of CO_2 and equivalent gases from industrial activities and business operations are measured.[48] Our first investment was in CarbonCure Technologies,[49] based in Nova Scotia, Canada, which has developed a technology for the $650 billion concrete and cement industry that introduces recycled CO_2 into fresh concrete to reduce its carbon footprint, crucially without impacting performance. Once injected, the CO_2 undergoes a mineralization process and becomes permanently embedded, resulting in economic and climate benefits for producers. As I write, the company had saved a total of 133,000 tons in CO_2 emissions, and delivered 1.832 million truckloads of CarbonCure concrete – while also reducing water usage and solid waste.

While these are early days, the company has already fitted equipment into more than 400 plants around the world. And as The Economist reported, its system has been used to construct buildings that include a new Amazon campus in Arlington, Virginia (Amazon is a shareholder in CarbonCure), and a General Motors electric vehicles assembly plant in Tennessee.[50]

(ii) Food/Ag-tech

Accounting for around 20 per cent of global GHGs today (some put the figure as high as 29 per cent[51]), and with demand only set to increase in order to keep pace with population growth, the food production and land use sector requires urgent transformation if net zero stands any chance of being met. Ag- and food-tech innovation companies are challenging incumbents and creating alternatives to intensive agricultural methods right across the spectrum, from soil to plate, through developing new forms of nutritious foods, urban/ vertical farms, so-called precision agriculture (i.e. technology-led farming) and carbon capture during the agricultural production process.

According to PitchBook data, since 2009 almost $23 billion has been ploughed into ag-tech start-ups globally.[52] Among the scores of notable companies in the space is Indigo Ag.[53] Founded in 2014, the Boston-headquartered firm, which at the time of writing had raised some $1.2 billion,[54] has – in its own words – four core offerings: 'biologicals' – which enables farmers to protect their crops and increase yield by using naturally occurring microbes extracted from plants; 'marketplace' – a technology platform that brings farmers and buyers together to sell grain more efficiently; 'transport' – which pledges to solve the pain points in a 'broken' logistics and transportation system that 'costs the agricultural industry billions a year'; and 'carbon'– which incentivizes farmers to adopt regenerative practices that are good for both farm and soil, such as adding cover crops, and reducing tillage (which we'll explore in depth in Chapter 6). Farmers can then get paid by generating verified carbon credits, via Carbon by Indigo, from showing increased soil organic matter or reduced GHG emissions.

One of the most fundamental issues to tackle in the sector is the overuse of synthetic fertilizers, which are a primary source of NO_2 emissions[55] (thanks in large part to the Haber–Bosch process, which converts hydrogen and nitrogen to produce ammonia – a technique I'll explore in greater depth in Chapter 7). Reliance on these and other synthetic agricultural inputs such as herbicides, pesticides and fungicides is adversely affecting our ecosystems, obliterating biodiversity, causing untold harm to our soils and under-soils, as well as ocean ecosystems, and, in a painfully sinister cycle, making farmers increasingly dependent on them all the while.

As argued in PwC's report, the development of new fertilizers with lower carbon footprints, and processes that reduce the level of GHG emitted in production, as well as in the use of current fertilizers, is a vital strand within ag-tech. Advances in biotechnology are enabling us to produce new solutions that increase soil and ecosystem health and ultimately make us healthier, too. They are helping to usher in a new form of agriculture that is regenerative instead of extractive. An example is Belgium-based Aphea.Bio,[56] which develops new and superior (naturally occurring) 'agricultural biologicals' to improve plant nutrient uptake and protect against disease without the need for fertilizers and pesticides. Instead of relying on harmful chemicals, Aphea.Bio uses biotechnology to identify naturally occurring microorganisms that stimulate plant growth and health for wheat and maize. The targeted application of these microorganisms can then boost the health and growth of these crops more naturally. This is not only better for the environment, but helps to restore the connection between the food on our plate, human health and the planet.

(iii) Consumer/Fast Fashion

While hard to measure because they encompass so many verticals, consumer goods from fridges to fast fashion have an outsized carbon footprint when tracked across the product's life cycle from resource extraction and manufacturer to retailer and disposal (all too often landfill). When considered alongside food production, consumer goods, across their lifespan, are estimated to account for more than 60 per cent of all GHG emissions, 80 per cent of water usage (mostly due to agriculture) and nearly two-thirds of tropical forest deforestation (again mostly due to agriculture).[57] But once more, start-ups are making a serious dent in these problems.

Fuelled by over $50 million of impact investment, New Jersey-based start-up Modern Meadow[58] – an Astanor portfolio company – works at the intersection of biotechnology and material science, and is taking on the $100 billion global leather industry by creating sustainable animal-free 'leather' from the plant-derived protein known as collagen.

Unsurprisingly given the complexity of the science and the scale of the challenge, the path to progress for Modern Meadow's team of scientists has been somewhat long, and not always linear. While the company had been 'very consistent on the problem (it) wanted to solve', from the outset the team 'had an iterative and evolving viewpoint on how technology might rise to the challenge', explains co-founder Andras Forgacs. They'd begun by growing skin cells in a laboratory to make an analogue of skin that could then be tanned to become an analogue of leather. But crucially, while it was interesting science, it simply wasn't workable in a commercial context, he says. 'Getting it to a level of performance that the consumer requires, that brands need, getting it to the level of scalability where you can actually make enough of it and achieve a price point that would be viable in the market, and getting it to a level of efficiency which would also support real sustainability benefits, was not obvious with that initial version of the technology.'

So they pivoted. Rather than skin, leather's main biological building block is actually collagen, Forgacs continues. 'Leather is really the extra-cellular matrix, the glue between cells that's primarily made of collagen – and it's the tanning and preservation of that matrix which makes leather. So we needed to figure out how to make collagen without the animals, and how to then structure that collagen so that we can make all kinds of collagen-based materials (from it).'

From 2015 the Modern Meadow team began working out how to produce collagen through fermentation – specifically, how to use yeast to make collagen, and then use collagen to make materials. But due to the protein's complexity, and its multiple varieties, while they were able to crack the technology, they couldn't produce it at the requisite scale and cost early on. 'And more to the point,' says Forgacs, 'we were also bottlenecked by (lack of) availability. Everything we want to do in terms of product development, material development, prototyping of shoes and bags, and all the sampling for brands, was bottlenecked by our ability to produce enough protein from fermentation tanks.'

Then in early 2020, realization dawned. 'While collagen is a special protein, it is representative of a category of proteins with a certain set of properties that can be used to make interesting materials. So we asked ourselves where else could we source these kinds of proteins by the metric ton?

'By broadening the aperture we were able to source similar proteins that have collagen-like functionality from a number of (agricultural) plants. We were then able to take those proteins, modify them, tune them, and use them as the raw materials, the secret sauce. And we can source them by the metric ton. That means that we can now make materials on a continuous production line, by the roll, and we can supply thousands of square metres of it.'

Thus produced at scale to make shoes, handbags, car seats and more, Modern Meadow's materials have huge potential to reconfigure an industry built on raising and slaughtering billions of animals a year, with profound implications both for needless animal suffering and the planet. Furthermore, the company's material technology is much more than just being an alternative to leather. Indeed, Forgacs describes it as a platform for making high-performance bio-based materials. 'The real impact of Modern Meadow's bio-alloy technology will be the combination of better performance, better scalability, and better sustainability that enables widespread accessibility and adoption.'

'Our goal is to become the Tetra Pak of sustainable packaging'

If leather is one market with an eye-watering carbon toll, plastics are another. With a daunting mission to eliminate one-time plastic use, sustainable packaging start-up Notpla[59] – slogan: 'We make packaging disappear' – has designed a replacement for plastic film made from brown seaweed, the ultimate renewable. When co-founder Pierre Paslier worked as a packaging engineer for L'Oréal, he came to the realization that of the tens of millions of plastic shampoo bottles and cosmetics cream jars, very few – especially of the cosmetics products – were ever recycled. 'I just had this nagging sense that the legacy of our era on Earth would be billions of plastic bottles, coffee cups and sachets,' Paslier recalls. 'And I wanted to do something about it.' Only he didn't yet know what.

So he quit L'Oréal and moved to London to study for a master's in Innovation Design Engineering at Imperial College and the Royal College of Art, where he embarked on a side project with his soon-to-be Notpla co-founder Rodrigo García González. In 2013, exploring the question of how nature might tackle food and liquid packaging waste, the pair began to experiment in their kitchen with natural ingredients. By trial and error, they eventually came up with a material that combined seaweed and plant extracts, which was not only robust and naturally biodegradable, but edible, too.

They built some 'very crude prototypes' of their early packaging product and, when the academic project (because that's all it was at that stage) was over, posted a video online about it.

'It went viral,' says Paslier. 'To our surprise, people were saying things like this could be an alternative to plastic, and it could be useful, for example, for marathon runners (when they snatch a cup of water), and festival-goers. And people really loved the idea of edible packaging. Remember: this was in 2014, before (Sir David Attenborough's) *Blue Planet II*; people were aware that we were using too much plastic, but there wasn't (yet) the emotional connection to the topic that there is now,' he says.

When they graduated, Paslier and González – convinced
that the large corporations responsible for most plastic waste
would not take a lead on the issue, and that change would
need to be driven by start-ups – joined a climate-tech-focused
incubator at Imperial and began work on the viability of their
idea. It was tough going for a couple of years, Paslier recalls.
They failed to raise any investment from angels or pre-seed
funds. But then, as a final roll of the dice, they launched
an equity crowdfunding campaign. It turned out to be an
inspired decision. 'It was much more participative,' he says.
'People could fund us for as little as £10, and buy shares in the
company. And after about nine months of pitching to funds
and getting zero commitment, in three days we raised one
million dollars and got a huge amount of visibility: one video on
Facebook (in 2017) got a hundred million views.'

From there the pair were able to put their first team together,
and set to work on the chemistry and manufacturing for
future projects. They were also able to start raising capital.
Fast-forward to today and Notpla – another Astanor portfolio
company – now has a catalogue of products ranging from
edible single-use packaging for liquids (for beverages, sauces,
juice, alcohol and condiments) to coating for previously
hard-to-recycle takeaway cartons, which makes them fully
biodegradable.

'Our goal is to become the Tetra Pak or Amcor of sustainable
packaging, not just with one solution but multiple solutions.
For example, Ooho (their edible material) is for instant
consumption, for marathons, festivals, cocktails and so on.
It has a short shelf life, and so we created a machine that
manufactures the product locally, close to the point of
consumption. So instead of having one big factory somewhere

in the world, we have multiple small hubs that can produce for the local environment. That way we can save on transportation, and we can basically enable those shorter shelf-life materials to play a role in reducing the use of plastic.'

'Climate tech … will produce eight to ten Teslas …'

These are just a few examples of the estimated (at the time of PwC's report) 1,200-plus climate tech start-ups that have been set up around the world, with more swelling their ranks by the week. As of 2020, forty-three had already been identified as unicorns with valuations of $1 billion plus, with Bill Gates predicting that the frenzy of activity in the climate tech space will ultimately, with the right government support, produce eight to ten Teslas, a Google, an Amazon and a Microsoft, despite 'a high failure rate'.[60]

The majority of new start-ups will indeed fail – a famous study from Harvard Business School found that around three-quarters of start-ups overall do not return money to investors[61] – and the risk is especially acute in a sector where runways are long and capital must be patient. But those odds are easily good enough to ensure impact investors will continue to back them – as they have been since the sector's earliest days. Beyond the obvious financial upside, collectively these disruptive technologies have the power to meet the climate challenge head-on and at a scale that makes 'quick fixes' like curbing air travel and talk of 'carbon footprints' look like the gesture politics they ultimately are.

Burning the library of life

Biodiversity and how to stem the tide of unprecedented loss

If nature in the purest sense of the word – the physical environment around us and the life that abounds within it – is Earth's most precious asset, then it is biodiversity that enables nature to be productive, resilient and adaptable.

What precisely do we mean by the word biodiversity? Coined in 1985 as a contraction of the phrase 'biological diversity', biodiversity, according to a colourful description from the American Museum of Natural History, 'refers to the variety of Life on Earth at all its levels, from genes to ecosystems, and can encompass the evolutionary, ecological, and cultural processes that sustain life'.[1]

For decades now, that variety of Life on Earth, in all its forms, has been caught in a spiral of decline.

A state of crisis

In his 1985 paper 'The Biological Diversity Crisis',[2] the late American scientist Edward O. Wilson memorably said that 'each species of higher organism is richer in information than a Caravaggio painting, a Bach fugue or any other great work of art'. Despite periodic attempts to estimate or extrapolate the number of species on Earth, Professor Wilson argued that the true extent of biological diversity remained essentially unmeasured.

He went on to address the question of why this issue matters. 'A species', he wrote, 'is a unique population of organisms, the terminus of a lineage that split off thousands or even millions of years ago. It has been hammered and shaped into its present form by mutations and natural selection, during which certain genetic combinations survived and reproduced differentially out of an almost inconceivably large number possible.'

It's estimated that there are around 8.7 million species on the planet, of which around 1.2 million have been identified and catalogued.[3] Experts believe as much as 86 per cent of land species and 91 per cent of marine species have yet to be discovered. Yet even when he wrote his paper almost four decades ago, Professor Wilson considered biological diversity to be in 'a state of crisis'. 'Quite simply,' he wrote, 'it is declining. Environmental destruction, a worldwide phenomenon, is reducing the number of species and the amount of genetic variation within individual species.'

Today it's clear the crisis Wilson described, when he sounded the alarm, now verges on the catastrophic. A comprehensive 2019 UN Report found that nature was 'declining at rates unprecedented in human history', and that 'the rate of species extinctions is accelerating'.[4] It estimated that 'around 1 million animal and plants species are now threatened with extinction, many within decades, more than ever before in human history'.

The authors of the report – who included 145 experts from fifty countries – found that 'the average abundance of native species in most major land-based habitats has fallen by at least 20%, mostly since 1900. More than 40% of amphibian species, almost 33% of reef-forming corals and more than a third of all marine mammals are threatened.' Other findings included that three-quarters of the land-based environment and about 66 per cent of the marine environment have been significantly altered by human actions, while more than a third of the world's land surface and nearly 75 per cent of freshwater resources are now devoted to crop or livestock production.

Insects, which form some 80 per cent of species on Earth[5] and have a significant impact on our world, face similar peril. Appearing at least 360 million years ago, they were among the first animals to colonize terrestrial ecosystems. Pollinators of our crops, they play an essential role in our food production, as well as in the cycling of organic matter and the maintenance of vertebrate populations. As I shall detail later, their rapid decline over the past few decades is nothing short of disastrous, representing 'the loss of essential, irreplaceable services to humanity'.[6]

COVID: a footnote?

According to the UN, there are five primary drivers of biodiversity decline. First, changes in land and sea use, such as deforestation. Second, direct exploitation of organisms – overfishing is a prime example. Third, climate change. Fourth, pollution. Fifth, invasive alien species.

And while it's not yet too late to slow and even reverse decline, and use nature sustainably, the impact of the loss of the planet's biodiversity – once vividly characterized as 'burning the library of life'[7] – has only recently been fully understood.

It's worth going into some detail about why, according to the World Health Organization (WHO), 'biodiversity underpins all life on Earth' – and how human health ultimately depends upon the planet's freshwater supply, food and sources of fuel, meaning that biodiversity loss can have direct and serious impacts on humanity if these are in short supply:[8]

- **It can threaten human wellbeing and even survival:**
  '… indirectly, changes in ecosystem services affect livelihoods, income, local migration, and, on occasion, may even cause or exacerbate political conflict'.

- **It can limit discovery of potential treatments for diseases and other health problems:** 'Biological diversity of microorganisms, flora and fauna provides extensive benefits for biological, health, and pharmacological sciences. … Biodiversity loss … means that we are losing, before discovery, many of nature's chemicals and genes …'

- **Biodiversity plays a critical role in human nutrition through its influence on world food production**, ensuring the sustainable productivity of soils and providing the genetic resources for all crops, livestock and marine species harvested for food. 'Intensified and enhanced food production through irrigation, use of fertilizer, plant protection (pesticides), or the introduction of crop varieties and cropping patterns affect biodiversity, and thus impact global nutritional status and human health.'

- **Infectious diseases:** Human activities are disturbing both the structure and functions of ecosystems, and altering native biodiversity. Such disturbances reduce the abundance of some organisms, cause population growth in others, modify the interactions among organisms and alter the interactions between organisms and their physical and chemical environments. Patterns of infectious diseases are sensitive to these disturbances. Major processes affecting infectious disease reservoirs and transmissions include: deforestation; land-use change; water management; resistance to pesticide chemicals used to control certain disease vectors; climate variability and change; migration and international travel and trade; and the accidental or intentional human introduction of pathogens.

Seen in this context and that of the unfolding crisis caused by issues such as deforestation, ocean degradation, GHG emissions and species over-exploitation, COVID-19 and the global pandemic, which had claimed over 6 million lives at the time of writing, might come to be viewed as no more than a small footnote in history by comparison.

Collectively we have failed to engage with nature sustainably, and the impact is already being keenly felt.

Pricing distortions

From the perspective of impact investors, nature's true worth to society – the real value of the various 'goods and services' it provides such as pollination – is simply not reflected in market prices. (Friends of the Earth, for example, reckon that it would cost EU farmers £1.8 billion to pollinate their crops without bees.[9]) This results in pricing distortions of 'services and assets', such as degraded soils and oceans, and gives rise to endless unaccounted for externalities.

Let's take an almond orchard as an example. Most types of almond tree require cross-pollination – which relies on bee colonies rather than wind pollination – to produce nuts. Let's say that next door to our almond grower's orchard is a farmer growing corn, who sprays his cornfields with insecticide during the brief window of time, of no more than a couple of weeks, in which the almond trees blossom. The net result of the inevitable insecticide drift is a decimated bee population on both properties, which means that the almond grower's trees probably won't produce any almond crop at all that year.

Now, that cost can be accounted for (or preferably avoided altogether of course). The almond grower can be compensated, or, at far greater expense, they might attempt to achieve pollination by another means, most often today by importing bee colonies from commercial beekeepers. Technology is also attacking the issue of vanishing bee populations from multiple perspectives:[10] farmers with the means at their disposal can drive large pollen-spraying rigs,[11] or, if so inclined, paint individual flowers with pollen using a paintbrush.[12] Researchers in Japan have even developed a bubble-based pollination method,[13] using 'flying robots equipped with bubble guns'.[14]

But just because these things are possible (or soon will be), there is currently no legal onus on the 'offending' farmer to ensure any of them happen today. What's more, the loss of biodiversity, which is multi-layered and far harder to measure, is likely, over time, to have a patchwork of impacts on the area; livelihoods may be lost, due to the inability to grow other crops also reliant on cross-pollination, with the health and even the survival of plants, insects and wildlife species, as well as people, also under threat. To put biodiversity loss in a global context, a study by the Boston Consulting Group found that the decline in ecosystem functionality already costs the global economy more than $5 trillion a year in the form of lost natural services.[15]

As with bees and pollen, so with earthworms and soil. A European Commission *Science for Environment* study found that 'Earthworms are proven to positively affect plant production, soil structure and pathogen control, and act as an important indicator of soil health.'[16] Indeed, soil health and soil biodiversity are interdependent, with earthworms usually the most abundant soil animal group among soil organisms present in agricultural soils, the study's authors continue. So, unsurprisingly, the threat to certain species of these 'ecosystem engineers' is already apparent in decreasing soil fertility. Surface-dwelling *epigeic* and/or subsoil-dwelling *anecic* earthworms were absent or rarely found in 42 per cent of sample fields, researchers in a pilot study in England found,[17] with their loss due mainly to intensive agricultural practices, such as excessive tillage.

What does this actually mean for soil health? According to a separate academic paper, '(Earthworms) are known to influence soil fertility by participating in important processes in soil such as soil structure regulation and organic matter dynamics. Earthworms also modify the microbial communities through digestion, stimulation and dispersion in casts.'[18]

Put in stark business terminology, nature affords us 'goods and services' such as these for free, when they are virtually priceless in pure monetary terms. Yet despite their steady erosion, no link is made between the P&L – the destructive actions of corporations, governments and individuals – and the balance sheet, nature's ultimate value.

Bottomless bounty

Instead we continue to behave as if Earth's balance sheet is infinite. The chef and author Dan Barber wrote in his 2016 book *The Third Plate: Field Notes on the Future of Food*[19] that it wasn't so long ago, 1883 in fact, that British biologist Thomas Henry Huxley, a contemporary of Darwin's, said that 'nothing we do seriously affects the number of fish in the sea'.

Huxley's notion of the oceans' inexhaustible bounty, widely believed at the time, came with the equally absurd and related idea that it 'was thought impossible to overburden the ocean with our waste'. Neither claim was supported by a shred of evidence, of course. As we know today, many of the toxic materials we use on land (e.g. the synthetic pesticides and fungicides used on golf courses[20]) end up leaching into the sea, resulting in more than 400 dead zones worldwide[21] – areas which do not have enough oxygen to support marine life.

Meanwhile, decades of destructive fishing[22] have led to the precipitous and near-terminal decline of fish species such as bluefin tuna and Grand Banks cod, as well as rapidly depleting other marine life including hundreds of thousands of seabirds and sea turtles, and tens of millions of sharks. Without action from humans, fish stocks are predicted to collapse by 2048.[23] 'Biodiversity is a finite resource, and we are going to end up with nothing left … if nothing changes,' Boris Worm, an assistant professor of marine conservation biology at Dalhousie University in Halifax, Nova Scotia, told *National Geographic*.

The idea that the oceans are a limitless resource to be plundered at will may have been roundly debunked, yet the attitude that if something is so expansive that it cannot effectively be measured prevails. We are borrowing ceaselessly – and blindly – from nature's balance sheet without knowing for sure when or how soon we will hit the bottom, and realize the barrel has been scraped almost bare.

Ecological deficit

Since the 1970s, humanity has been in a position of global ecological deficit, reaching the point where it would require the equivalent of 1.6 Earths[24] today to satisfy humanity's demands from our planet's fragile ecosystems. The international research organization Global Footprint Network even pinpoints Earth Overshoot Day[25] each year – 'the date when humanity's demand for ecological resources and services in a given year exceeds what Earth can regenerate in that year'. In 2021, that day was 29 July (almost a month earlier than the preceding year), resulting in a deficit funded by chipping away at Earth's balance sheet.

To stabilize, let alone reverse, this pattern, our relationship with nature needs to move with alacrity from being extractive to regenerative. Across the world pioneers and innovators are making headway at protecting the planet's remaining biodiversity and transitioning to regenerative practices. It's work that must be scaled up by orders of magnitude to avoid an ecological tailspin.

Aquaculture

French start-up Ÿnsect farms insects (Molitor mealworm larvae) to produce high-quality and sustainable food for aquaculture – the farming of fish, crustaceans and mollusks, etc. – as well as pet nutrition. As investors in the company for a while now, my team at Astanor measures Ÿnsect's progress in a number of ways including by tracking how 'regenerative' the company is – specifically how it contributes towards healthy soils and oceans.

Ÿnsect is regenerative in three key ways. First, it helps preserve ocean fish stocks. Currently around 25 per cent of rapidly declining fish stocks – including smaller fish, which are among the most overfished – are processed into animal feed. Ÿnsect provides a sustainable alternative protein, which helps stem ocean depletion, while also reducing the fishing industry's carbon footprint by decreasing the number of trawlers that go out to fish.

Second, the company has helped preserve biodiversity through its 'Rewilding the World' programme, in association with ASPAS (Association for the Protection of Wild Animals) and WWF (World Wildlife Fund), which offsets the start-up's footprint by returning at least as much land to nature – at the time of writing, 370 hectares have been preserved in this way.

Third, Ÿnsect's fertilizer ŸnFrass, made from the mealworm's guano – a by-product of mealworm protein, produced as part of its zero-waste commitment – has been certified as organic, with a study already showing promising results on rapeseed, wheat and corn,[26] and appearing 'to improve the biological properties of soil'.[27] Critically, by using Ynfrass instead of traditional petroleum-derived fertilizers, Ÿnsect customers are saving a huge amount of CO_2 and therefore have a net negative carbon footprint.

Pesticides and biodiversity

We know that agricultural pesticides and fungicides have a major impact upon soil health and biodiversity. A 2021 peer-reviewed study, 'Pesticides and Soil Invertebrates: A Hazard Assessment',[28] found that 'pesticides widely used in American agriculture pose a grave threat to organisms needed for healthy soil, biodiversity and the fight against climate change. We found that in 71 per cent of cases studied, pesticides kill or harm soil invertebrates like earthworms, ants, beetles and ground-nesting bees.

'We found negative effects across all studied pesticide classes, which shows that pesticides – as a set of chemical poisons – pose a clear hazard to soil life and are incompatible with healthy soil.'[29] Furthermore the Food and Agriculture Organization (FAO) of the UN believes that '33% of (the world's) land is moderately to highly degraded due to erosion, salinization, compaction, acidification, and chemical pollution of soils'.[30] But it also found that the effects can be rolled back, and once again technology is on hand to help unpick the damage. Advancements in biotechnology are enabling us to produce new solutions that increase soil and ecosystem health and ultimately make us healthier, too. They are also ushering in a new form of regenerative agriculture.

There are a few companies in Europe tackling this issue. Potsdam's Stenon is taking soil analysis out of the laboratory and giving it directly to farmers in the field. Its accurate, real-time soil technology provides farmers with insights in seconds into how the soil is functioning and what needs to be done to improve it using more than 5,000 data points per measurement. Ireland-headquartered MicroGen Biotech, meanwhile, is developing technology that uses natural microbes to block the uptake of heavy metals by crops on land. The product works to break down pollutants and support the growth of good bacteria to revitalize the land, without the use of destructive chemicals. Then there's US-based Trace Genomics, which has built a scalable soil microbiome test to help farmers predict soil health and crop quality, using a combination of DNA sequencing and machine learning. These insights equip growers with a better grasp of the parameters affecting production, helping them to make clearer decisions and get more value out of their land. This could not have been possible a decade or so ago, but the development of data processing and machine learning across the agri-food system offers us a glimpse of future possibilities.

Regeneration

'We've spent most of the last century in agriculture trying to advise farmers on how to kill the things they don't want in their soil'

In his 2017 book *Growing a Revolution: Bringing Our Soil Back to Life*, Professor David R. Montgomery describes how agricultural practices over centuries have degraded soil's fertility by stripping it of the organic matter essential to its productivity. While researching the book, he travelled the world, from Kansas to Kenya, interviewing regenerative farmers and testing their soil. 'It took about six months to visit farmers around the world. And it was not an unbiased sample of farmers: I went to visit the farmers who had been very successful at restoring fertility to their land, because I'd already written a book about how land is degraded, and I didn't need to learn a whole lot more about how to do that. Instead I visited farmers from small scale subsistence farmers in equatorial Africa to very large industrialized farms in the United States that are regenerative, despite being industrialized, because of the way they do things that is actually rebuilding soil fertility.'

So what was it that the farmers who were very successful in these different settings – different climates, different regions of the world with different technologies and different sizes of farms – had in common?

'In *Growing a Revolution* I characterize it as "Ditch the plow", "Cover up" and "Grow diversity",' Professor Montgomery continues. 'What they had in common was that they've gone to no-till farming, so they are no longer ploughing, and adopted cover crops as a central tenet of their farming practices, which means that they always kept living plants growing in the soil at all times. So there's now no bare ground. And the third necessary leg of the regenerative stool was looking at a greater diversity of crops. So they weren't just growing corn and soybeans. They were growing at least four or five different crops in a rotation, and some of them got most of their diversity in their cover crops. One of the farmers, for example, sold wheat, corn and soybeans, but he grew a lot of different cover crops – ten to twelve different varieties of cover crops, often in the same field in between his cash crops.

'That combination of minimal disturbance, keeping the land covered with growing plants, and a diversity of growing plants either in a mix of plants or in a rotation, is a recipe for doing something that's at the heart of building soil fertility: and that's supporting microbial life, the beneficial life in the soil.'

The subtitle of *Growing a Revolution, Bringing Our Soil Back to Life*, literally refers to putting beneficial life back in the soil, he says. 'We've spent most of the last century in agriculture trying to advise farmers on how to kill the things they don't want in their soil, when they would be better advised to figure out how to promote the life they should want in the soil first, and then deal with pests and pathogens if need be using agrichemicals. But what the experience of the farmers I visited showed was that their pest problems pretty much went away once they adopted those three principles because the beneficial life out-competed the detrimental life.'

Repairing biodiversity in this way, as part of a generational shift towards a new type of regenerative agriculture, is a prime example of the impact investor's mission, where quick fixes and interim solutions are jettisoned in favour of sustainability and long-term measurable outcomes. As we'll see, this approach results in food that is both more nourishing and delicious; better for our health and for the planet. But before we look at how innovation in technology and biosciences are helping to bring this change about, let's step back for a moment to consider the startling gulf between the food we believe we're eating today and the rather less palatable reality.

Farming
We are what our food ate

'Fat-free!' 'Farm-fresh!' 'Low-salt!' 'Multi-grain!'

When we casually toss a packet or carton into our shopping cart, perhaps only glimpsing the reassuring words printed on the label, we think we know what we're buying. Or at least we assume we have a general idea of whether a product is, broadly speaking, 'healthy' or not. The reality is that we emphatically do not. Labels don't simply mislead consumers, they bamboozle and trick us, and play on our weaknesses.

A rule of thumb: if it sounds too good to be true, it probably is. Take that enticing packet of 'fat-free' chocolate chip cookies. Chances are each cookie is loaded with as much sugar, and may contain as many calories, as the full-fat variety. Or a favourite 'sugar-free' snack. Yes, it may contain less than 0.5 grams of sugars per serving (the definition in the US[1]), but it is probably packed with calories and carbohydrates from other sources (not to mention bloat-inducing 'sugar alcohols').[2]

'Multi-grain' bread may conjure up images of a healthy artisan loaf, but all that misleading term means is that it has been made with more than one type of grain. It may well have had anything of genuine nutritional value, such as fibre, removed during processing.[3] It may even have been made from refined white flour, then dyed with food colouring in order to appear healthy. (Yes, that does happen.)[4]

Research in the US has found that food manufacturers add sugar to 74 per cent of packaged foods sold in supermarkets, and not just to desserts, but also to pasta sauces, ready meals and seemingly 'healthy' fruit juices, too.[5] Sugar comes in many forms, of course. In fact there are at least sixty-one different names for sugar listed on food labels, ranging from the obvious (cane sugar, caramel, brown sugar) to the downright obscure (maltose, refiner's syrup, dextrin, evaporated cane extract).[6] No surprise, then, that the average American consumes, often without knowing it, an estimated 57 pounds of added sugar annually – seventeen teaspoons a day, at least twice the recommended amount[7] – and that two-thirds of the population are classified as overweight or obese, resulting in ballooning healthcare costs of up to $210 billion a year to the US taxpayer.[8]

It's easy to dismiss mislabelling as unscrupulous marketing by Big Food companies, and to believe that if only consumers would spend a fraction of the time trawling through the fine print and researching the 'true' ingredients on the label that they spend eating, then it's entirely possible to sift the unhealthy, obesity- and coronary-heart-disease-causing food from the healthy variety. If only. The entire issue of mislabelling, though often scandalous, obscures a deeper and more significant malaise: namely, our tenuous and often illusory grasp of what is really in our food, even the organic variety.

'Go to work on an egg'

In the 1950s and 1960s, the UK's unimaginatively named Egg
Marketing Board ran an advertising campaign which included
TV spots featuring one of Britain's best-loved comedians of
the day, Tony Hancock. The commercials, which ran just a few
years after eggs came off rationing in post-war Britain,[9] carried
the catchy strapline 'Go to work on an egg'.[10] Often wrongly
attributed exclusively to the novelist Fay Weldon – it actually
came from the creative team she led at ad agency Ogilvy &
Mather at the time – the slogan was based on the premise that
the nutritional benefits of eggs set you up for the day ('Start
the day right with eggs,' Hancock's on-screen wife declares in
the ad).[11] However, eggs, even pricey organic ones, may not
always be as healthy as they seem.

According to the UK Soil Association guidelines,[12] the criteria
required for an egg to be certified as organic include the
stipulation that 'poultry must have continuous and easy
daytime access to an outdoor range covered with suitable
vegetation'. In practice this means that each laying hen is
allowed a minimum of 10 square metres of space outside
(compared with 4 square metres for hens reared to EU organic
and free-range standards). Another requirement is that hens
are fed a GM-free diet, and that outdoor foraging enables
organic chickens 'to eat a variety of plants, grubs and insects
...' Under these standards, organic hens therefore take in a lot
of omega-3 fatty acids in their natural diets from the fresh herbs,
flax and linseed they forage.

Now the reason eggs are actually good for us is that they are a
natural, concentrated source of DHA (docosahexaenoic acid),
a long-chain omega-3 fatty acid.[13] But as the leading French
agronomist Pierre Weill told me, having 'organic' printed on

an egg-box label is no guarantee of nutritional value. 'As an eater of eggs in countries like France, when you see the words "free range" or "organic", you imagine the laying hen is eating grass, worms and other little insects, and that she's happy, and because she's happy she will produce eggs with a very high nutritional value. But it's not true because (the reality is) this organic hen is probably living in a barn with thousands of other laying hens, and she doesn't go outside very often, and she's eating industrial food made mainly from organic soya bean, often from China, and organic corn, often from Ukraine.' In fact when you actually dig down and measure the nutrient content of eggs resulting from the set-up and diet Weill describes, they are likely to contain poor levels of omega-3, but high concentrations of omega-6.

Thanks to 1982 Nobel Prize-winners Bergström, Samuelsson and Vane,[14] we know that humans cannot synthetize omega-3 or omega-6, vital as they are to our health, so we must acquire them from foods such as fish, vegetable oils, certain nuts such as walnuts, flax seeds, flaxseed oil and leafy vegetables.[15] However, while we need both of them, their ratio must stay within a certain range. The generally recommended ratio for omega-3 to omega-6 is 1:4 or less, certainly not the 1:10 ratio of the typical American diet. Omega-6-rich diets are known to accelerate inflammation, while diets rich in omega-3 fatty acids have beneficial anti-inflammatory effects, which make us more resistant to diseases.

Therefore even if you consume an egg stamped with the word organic – and even if the laying hen was fed with an organic diet (albeit one imported from China and Ukraine) – you cannot be sure whether you are getting the omega-3 you need, or the excess omega-6 you don't.

Furthermore, whether we are talking about the diets of hens or humans, or indeed soil, diversity must always be paramount, Weill continues. 'If a hen eats a little grass, a little alfalfa, a little linseed, a little lupine, a little pea, and so on, of course, all these different foods will provide different nutrients for the hen and these different nutrients will also ultimately benefit the eater's health. But if a hen eats only corn and soya, even if it's organic and non-GMO, it will not be good for either hen or human.

'Diversity is probably the single best thing for building health. It's true for humans, it's true for animals, and its true for the soils too. If you grow every year the same crop – wheat, followed by wheat and then more wheat, the soil will become tired. If you feed a hen, or a cow, with corn and soy all the days of her life, she will be tired too, and she will not (provide) nutritious eggs. I once had a professor of biochemistry and he would explain very complicated things about desaturase enzymes, omega-6, omega-3 etc., and at the end of his lecture, he said, "Now I must pay tribute to the person who taught me so much about nutrition – my grandmother. She said *Eat a little piece of everything and you will be in good health.* It's a basic rule."'

As Weill says, the same logic applies to plant-derived food, too. Healthy soil teems with bacteria, fungi, algae, protozoa, nematodes and other tiny creatures. Such organisms play an important role in plant health. Soil bacteria produce natural antibiotics that help plants resist disease. Fungi assist plants in absorbing water and nutrients. Together, these bacteria and fungi are known as 'organic matter'. The more organic matter in a sample of soil, the healthier that soil is.

Although crops can, of course, be grown in exhausted soils, they barely survive on a 'fast-food' diet of synthetic fertilizers, artificially protected from competing plants by herbicides and from attacking insects by pesticides, and often reliant on intensive irrigation. Crucially, their roots cannot extract from the soil the micronutrients (both primary and secondary[16]) that make them as nutritious as they used to be when we learned over millennia that cereals, vegetables and fruit are good for our health as part of a healthy, balanced diet – or indeed the diets of the animals we ate.

If crops are grown on a 'fast-food' diet, deprived of the micronutrients required for healthy and productive growth, then it follows that we, as consumers (or 'eaters' as Weill describes us), are not getting the benefits from our diets that we think we are. Even if the food is labelled organic or 'bio' (as it is in France).

Or, to put it another way, we are not what we eat, but more accurately, *we are what our food ate*.

Full transparency

Awareness of what has come to be called sustainable agriculture and the importance of healthy soils – and of farmers themselves – in the food ecosystem has been growing for a while, driven in part by landmark books such as Eric Schlosser's *Fast Food Nation* (2002) and *The Omnivore's Dilemma* by Michael Pollan, published four years later. These books, alongside popular documentaries such as Morgan Spurlock's 2004 hit *Super Size Me*, trained the spotlight on industrial food production, revealing the often grotesque underbelly of America's processed food industry, how vast corporations have a stranglehold on the American diet and how consumers are steadily paying the price.

Among Schlosser's most astounding revelations were the laboratories where artificial flavours for French fries, savoury snacks such as potato chips and crackers, breakfast cereals and even toothpastes are designed by 'food technologists'.[17] Pollan's acclaimed book zeroed in on, among many other things, the ubiquity of corn and corn derivatives, and how 'high-fructose corn syrup (HFCS)' had become the leading source of sweetness in the American diet, found everywhere from soft drinks to ketchup, mustard, bread, cereal, hot dogs and hams, helping entrench the US's obesity epidemic in the process. 'There are some forty-five thousand items in the average American supermarket and more than a quarter of them now contain corn. This goes for the nonfood items as well – everything from the toothpaste and cosmetics to the disposable diapers, trash bags, cleansers, charcoal briquettes, matches, and batteries, right down to the shine on the cover of the magazine that catches your eye by the checkout: corn.'[18]

These and other revelations, which served to show how industrialized systems, churning out highly processed products, had all but severed the link between soil, 'traditional farming' and the plate, led growing numbers of consumers to search for healthier alternatives. As Gary Kleppel phrased it in his book *The Emergent Agriculture: Farming, Sustainability and the Return of the Local Economy* (2014), 'Consumers are now beginning to question the notion of food as a commodity, and to realize the production of safe, nutritious food requires respect for the soil, for living organisms, for ecosystems, and for farmers.'

One powerful way to help restore this link is absolute clarity about the ingredients of the food on our plate – whether we're talking about a ready meal, organic eggs or even a humble piece of fresh fruit. For Pierre Weill, who is also co-president of Bleu-Blanc-Coeur – a French association created in 2000, which 'promotes responsible agriculture with the objective of improving the nutritional and environmental quality of our food'[19] – such clarity boils down to three elements: soil diversity, the nutritional quality of animal/plant diet and, just as importantly, measurement.

On this last point, Weill recalls meeting fierce resistance from some organic farmers to the very notion that the nutritional quality of their products should be measured. 'I have been meeting organic farmers for forty years,' he says. 'They are very nice people, they really believe in what they do, they really believe in their mission. But they are attached to what they call "obligation of means", not "obligation of results". The nutritional quality of an organic egg can be measured. But they don't like (that idea) because they believe they treat their laying hens in the best way they can, so their eggs will be of good quality. But that's not enough today, because it's quite easy to measure the nutritional quality of an egg, a salad, of every farm product, and that ability can build a new relationship between producer and consumer.'

He warms to his theme: 'Measurement is really the key for human health and the environment, but also in the relationship between the health of animals and soil health. When you improve the diversity in the soil, you improve the quality of the soil, the life in the soil. The worms and fungi and so on will work better and will provide more nutrients from the soil. Plants will be able to synthesize more antioxidants, polyphenols, flavonoids and beta-carotene. And when animals and humans, at the very end of the food chain, eat those plants, they will be in measurably better health.'

Similarly, in an ideal world, before we buy food or drink in the supermarket or online, being able to know the precise composition of our purchases – rather than the theoretical levels based on average predicted contents that appear on labels, nutrition apps and the other static information sources we rely on at the moment – would surely be transformative. Food data project Teak Origin, spun out of MIT's Media Lab, has worked on this problem. By using a combination of analytical chemistry, optical spectroscopy and machine learning, among other tools, the team were able to analyse the fine components of food items, starting with fresh produce.

Based on the premise that no two items of food have identical nutritional value – even if they are superficially the same – the researchers produced a study which found, for example, that for a series of products bought on the same day from a range of supermarkets in the same US city in early 2021, the nutrient quantity of fresh produce would vary widely, even if they were sold as the 'same fruit'. Red grapes, for example, are sought after because of their reported levels of anthocyanin – a pigmented class of compounds with antioxidant activity that are found exclusively in the skin of table grapes. Strong concentrations are therefore an indicator of high quality. Among batches tested that day, their level fluctuated from 2.98 milligrams per 100 grams at one supermarket chain, to 34.28 milligrams per 100 grams in another – an 11.5 times difference for the same fruit.

The study also found equivalent nutritional quality differences between apples, avocados, strawberries, bananas, blueberries – with vitamins, antioxidants, selenium, potassium and so on varying by factors of one to twenty times from one source to another, largely because of the soil they grew in, but also because of the time it took for them to reach retailers, as many of these micronutrients decay over time. More often than not the more nutritious items were not more expensive

Figure 1

than the others – which indicates how our societies don't value nutritional quality per se; in fact we actively deprioritize it. This is because we still look at food strictly as energy going into our body in the form of lipids, carbs and proteins.

'Fuel and building blocks'

In her fascinating article 'Eating as Dialogue, Food as Technology: Food is being reconceived as a currency of communication',[20] Berggruen Institute fellow, historian and sociologist Hannah Landecker wrote that a hundred years ago, 'at the height of the German chemical industry's global dominance', food was considered to be 'fuel and building blocks'. This resulted in 'a very particular kind of eating body', wrote Landecker, 'a motor built from smaller units that burns energy to move'. She went on to cite a well-known 1926 illustration, *Der Mensch als Industriepalast* (*Man as Industrial Palace*) by German physician Fritz Kahn, which depicts the body 'as a chemical plant in which food is being broken down in the intestinal tract and processed through the liver to power the muscles'.

At the time, continued Landecker, 'the body as a factory envisioned by Kahn … (reflected) an industrial society based on manufacturing and the harnessing of chemical transformation for productivity'.

Although that image was created nearly a century ago, the thinking behind it cast a long shadow. Even today, because of that image of the human body, the food system has been predicated on producing calories (= energy) at the expense of all other quality attributes including nutrition. The underlying reason is that since the end of the Second World War, as concerns about food supply and security were both legitimate and urgent, the world designed a very efficient system for delivering cheap calories in abundance.

In doing so, however, we failed to make this system efficient at producing affordable nutrients.

Until very recently, policymakers and international organizations were only concerned about whether the world would be able to create sufficient calories to feed a growing population expected to peak at almost 10 billion by 2050.[21] These concerns were entirely legitimate, of course, given that as recently as 2018, according to the WHO, an estimated 820 million people went hungry[22] – and that number is growing. But most food poverty is caused by political issues leading to social turmoil. Food aid arrives in large enough quantities in seaports and airports in most of the world's most deprived areas, where malnutrition thrives. The real scandal is that this aid often does not make its way to those who need it most. As the Anglo-American Nobel Prize-winning economist Angus Deaton succinctly phrased it: 'To get to the powerless, you have to go through the powerful.'[23]

Meanwhile, obesity has almost tripled since 1975, with 39 per cent of adults classified as either overweight or obese[24] – and at risk of developing dangerous diet-related chronic diseases, including type 2 diabetes and cardiovascular disease, and leaving them more susceptible to serious illness or death from COVID-19. Obesity is invariably triggered by excessive calorific intake in the form of ultra-processed foods and beverages, which contain excess sugars, coupled with a deficiency of fibre, trace minerals, antioxidants, fatty acids, and so on, all of which are to be found in genuinely fresh food.

Bluntly, plants growing in exhausted soil, devoid of micronutrients, offer ever-diminishing returns of essential nutrients to the animals and people further along the food chain. Furthermore, as ever-increasing numbers join the global middle classes and cook less fresh food from scratch, they are more likely to eat ultra-processed meat and vegetables in the form of ready meals or pre-prepared food, from which antioxidants and fatty acids are often extracted as a consequence of extending shelf life, and which fall far short of the nutrition levels required to maintain reasonable human health.

I will go on to argue that the solution for improved diets, healthier lives and a sustainable planet lies not only in restoring soil quality, but also in re-establishing the delicate symbiosis between crops, farm animals and soil – while also bringing much-needed transparency to the food-ag industry to help people make the right decisions regarding their diet. However, first we need to explore how the global intensive farming system has long since surpassed the limits of sustainability, and utterly fails the impact investor's test of achieving measurable beneficial social and environmental outcomes.

Industrial food for thought

'It's not the cow, it's the how'

Battery hens each confined to a space smaller than an A4 sheet of paper.[1] Sows that are trapped between two rails so that they cannot turn around to tend to their piglets.[2] Antibiotics used more heavily (outside the EU) in farm animals than people,[3] leading to the seepage of drug-resistant bacteria into the human food chain …[4] With an estimated two out of every three animals intensively farmed (over 50 billion a year globally[5]) to provide the world with an endless production line of 'cheap' protein, the horrors of the industrial farming of livestock – which the author Yuval Noah Harrari has described as 'perhaps the worst crime in history'[6] – are well documented, as is its impact on human health from cancers to heart disease.[7]

What's certainly less widely known, however, is that industrialized arable farming has a similarly super-sized impact not just on our health (which I'll return to shortly), but also on our planet, especially with regard to climate change.[8] To understand why, let's focus for a moment on corn, the Godzilla of the American diet, omnipresent in the food chain from animal feed to sodas to disposable diapers. To return for a moment to Michael Pollan's *The Omnivore's Dilemma* once more: 'Corn is what feeds the steer that becomes the steak. Corn feeds the chicken and the pig, the turkey and the lamb, the catfish and the tilapia and increasingly, even the salmon, a carnivore by nature that the fish farmers are reengineering to tolerate corn. The eggs are made of corn. The milk and cheese and yogurt, which once came from dairy cows that grazed on grass, now typically come from Holsteins that spend their working lives indoors tethered to machines, eating corn ...

'Head over to the processed foods (aisle) and you find ever more intricate manifestations of corn. A chicken nugget, for example, piles corn upon corn: what chicken it contains consists of corn, of course, but so do most of a nugget's other constituents, including the modified corn starch that glues the thing together, the corn flour in the batter that coats it, and the corn oil in which it gets fried ...'

The net effect of monoculture agriculture – where only one type of crop is grown continuously on a field or farm – and the dominance of commodity crops such as corn, soy/soya bean and wheat, is depleted and degraded soils. Soils which are stripped of their micronutrients, yet awash with petrochemical-based fertilizers and pesticides, with their proven links to cancers and other diseases among farm workers, local populations and consumers.[9] Furthermore, the vast majority of commodity crops are used to feed and fatten livestock, while only a small fraction of the corn grown in the US is actually consumed by humans, and much of that is used to manufacture high-fructose corn syrup.[10] In Europe, meanwhile, the proportion of crops available on the Continent that are fed to livestock stands respectively at 58 per cent for cereals and

67 per cent for oilseed/protein crops – with most of the latter imported from South America in the form of soybean meal.[11] as we have already encountered with our plant-based burger example.

Against a backdrop where 24 billion tons of fertile land are lost to desertification every year anyway,[12] primarily as a result of human activity and climatic variations, intensive production of crops – which are then shipped often thousands of miles across the world – alongside related industrial farming practices and land-use represent around 25 per cent of all global GHG emissions. Industrial agriculture is extremely harmful to the environment in other ways, too, including in its demands on freshwater (agriculture accounts for a staggering 70 per cent of water withdrawals worldwide), its polluting run-offs into the oceans and the biodiversity loss it causes. I mentioned 'dead zones' in Chapter 5. The Gulf of Mexico's infamous summer dead zone, for example, where oxygen levels are too low to support most marine life, is directly linked to industrial farming in the Great Plains of Canada and the US, through the drainage of the great Mississippi/Missouri basins, as well as the human and animal sewage that is pumped into the Gulf.[13] In Brittany, north-west France, toxic coastal algae blooms,[14] which environmentalists link to nitrates in fertilizers used by the intensive pig, poultry and dairy industries, have been linked to at least two human fatalities.

Caught in a race to produce ever-larger volumes to satisfy the premise that value = quantity, industrial agriculture has degraded the land to the point of making farming unsustainable without record volumes of chemical fertilizers and pesticides. This in turn has meant that farmers require ever more sophisticated and expensive inputs (fertilizers, pesticides, etc.) to achieve the same yields, leaving only those who are able to scale their acreage to amortize the fixed costs to be able to continue to make ends meet. Meanwhile, those famers who have made the switch to higher value crops derived from regenerative agriculture are faced with the near-insurmountable task of selling them at the necessary premium price point because nutrient density remains undervalued in our current commodity-based marketplace. And, as long as the nutritional value of food ingredients, starting with plant crops, is not fully exposed to consumers and regulators, the agri-food systems will remain stuck on producing the cheapest possible calories instead of great nutrients at the cheapest possible cost.

Soil, revisited

To dig a little deeper into how the food we eat has been impacted by intensive farming we first need to return to the topic of soil, which directly or indirectly provides us with about 95 per cent of our food.[15] As I described in Chapter 1, from the earliest eras humanity has teetered on the brink of famine due to the unpredictability and unreliability of our food supply. Soil quality has therefore remained at the heart of our quest for survival, and, as Professor Montgomery argues, entire civilizations have collapsed when soils became exhausted, degraded or eroded.

It took time for the role of soil to be fully understood. For many centuries farmers practised crop rotations and enriched the soil with animal (and human) manure, or bird and bat guano. Both practices were empirical, proven ways of restoring levels of nitrogen as well as potassium and phosphorus to the soil, as these essential mineral elements each play a key role in plant nutrition and growth, alongside water and sunlight.

Everything changed in 1908, however, when two German chemists – the previously mentioned Fritz Haber and Carl Bosch – invented a way to synthesize ammonia from nitrogen and hydrogen in a factory, freeing the world from the bottleneck of animal manure production to produce fertilizers in very large quantities and therefore enable farming at scale. Up until that point if a society needed more produce to feed its population, effectively the only answer was to acquire more land. By converting hydrogen and nitrogen into ammonia,[16] not only did the chemists bring about the mass production of fertilizers and therefore the ramping up of agricultural yields, but they also ignited a global population spike. According to one estimate, the Haber–Bosch process is likely to have enabled the lives of at least 3–3.5 billion people today.[17]

Yet this scientific and societal breakthrough came at considerable environmental cost. First, it's reckoned to account for up to 2.4 per cent of total global emissions on its own[18] (producing ammonia in factories requires an enormous amount of heat, which means burning large quantities of fossil fuel, specifically natural gas, which releases billions of tons of CO_2 into the atmosphere) and consumes 1 per cent of the world's total energy production.[19]

The second, perhaps even heftier, price tag from the widespread use of synthetic fertilizers has been caused by the underlying assumption that soils were just inert substrates that simply needed NPK (the soil life 'trinity' of nitrogen, phosphorous and potassium) to enable plant growth. That ignored the importance of microbial soil life as well as the equally vital mycelium interaction with plant roots. (Only mycelium has the capacity to break down rocks into the minute mineral compounds that are needed by plants to live and grow and that can be absorbed essentially via the mycorrhizae, the interface between the plants roots and the mycelium. In exchange for providing plants with mineral compounds such as phosphorus, potassium, selenium, iron and so on, plants provide mycelium with the energy they pump from the sun via photosynthesis that the mushroom kingdom has never been able to master itself.)

This oversimplification regarding NPK, typical of the late-nineteenth-century Western European school of engineering mindset, led to the abandonment of ancestral wisdom, developed over generations, of crop rotations that allow soils to be restored over multiple seasons by alternating between growing plants that take nitrogen out of the soil, with plants that deposit nitrogen back into it.

Industrial-scale fallout

It's worth remembering that the ambition behind industrialized farming was a noble one. It first came about in the US after the First World War as a way of combatting global hunger and making the food supply more robust, secure and plentiful. In an effort to eliminate inefficiencies and banish memories of the food shortages of the Great Depression, wartime mechanization technology was applied to farming, alongside the use of chemicals for fertilizers and pesticides, and non-therapeutic antibiotics.[20]

Over the decades since, as industrial farming became the established paradigm in the West, small and medium-sized farms were gradually replaced by fewer 'mega-farms'. The number of American farms more than halved from 4.78 million in 1954[21] to just 2.05 million by 2017.[22] Today it's estimated that just 20 per cent of farms control nearly 70 per cent of US farmland. Globally that figure is even worse: the largest 1 per cent of farms operate more than 70 per cent of the world's farmland and are integrated into the corporate 'commodity' food system, while over 80 per cent are smallholdings that are generally excluded from profitable global food chains, according to a report from the Land Inequality Initiative.[23]

Consolidation and industrialization have undoubtedly led to inexpensive food – or, more accurately, inexpensive calories – in the West in particular (Americans spend just 6.4 per cent[24] of their household income on food), and, globally, between 1960 and 2015, agricultural production more than trebled, according to the UN Environment Program (UNEP) 'resulting in an abundance of low-cost fare and averting global food shortages'.[25] In which case, shouldn't we regard industrial farming – on its own terms, at least – as an outright success?

The answer is a resounding no. For one thing, as we've seen, with over 820 million people going hungry globally,[26] it certainly hasn't solved world food poverty. And with the global population predicted to rise to almost 10 billion people by 2050 (although growth is now flattening out[27]), the picture becomes muddier still. While the world can theoretically produce sufficient cheap, ultra-processed calories to feed 10 billion (although whether the 'food' would reach those who need it most remains moot), as more and more see their income rise and the global middle classes consequently expand, demand for animal proteins would soar – on a scale that would be unlikely to be met – with an accompanying disastrous rise in GHG emissions.

Then there's the value-for-money counter-argument. Once again official figures fail to take into account the true and complete cost of industrial farming. According to one estimate from research undertaken on behalf of the Food and Agriculture Organization (FAO) of the UN, the true cost to the environment encompassing GHG emissions, air and water pollution, and biodiversity loss – as well as the cost of repair – amounts to as much as $3 trillion a year, with crop production alone costing some $1.15 trillion annually, about 170 per cent of its production value.[28] As an impact investor looking for measurable outcomes, beyond profit, a complete true cost accounting (TCA) of the impact of industrial farming production and output would cover not only the above (i.e. GHG emissions, air and water pollution, and biodiversity loss), but also water usage, soil depletion, ocean degradation, as well as the health costs linked to dietary diseases.

Other fallouts from industrial farming, according to the UNEP,[29] include the facilitation of the spread of viruses from animals to humans, where intensive livestock farming 'can effectively serve as a bridge for pathogens'. It has also been linked to zoonotic diseases.

Next, thanks to the practice of feeding antimicrobials to livestock – not just to prevent or treat disease, but to accelerate growth – industrial agriculture is contributing to the gathering storm of antimicrobial resistance. It's estimated that drug-resistant diseases already cause around 700,000 deaths a year, including 230,000 deaths from multidrug-resistant tuberculosis.[30] That figure could rise explosively to 10 million deaths annually by 2050 – with about 2.4 million deaths in high-income countries between 2015 and 2050 – threatening to unravel a century of progress in health, according to the WHO, and ushering in a 'post-antibiotic era', where people die of common infections and minor injuries.

I have already covered the link between the use of fertilizers and pesticides and diseases such as cancer. Some pesticides used in intensive agriculture have been shown to act as endocrine disruptors,[31] disrupting human reproductive and sexual development, with human fetuses, infants and children showing greater susceptibility than adults. Meanwhile, nitrate, agriculture's most common chemical contaminant, according to the UNEP, is a cause of 'blue baby syndrome', a potentially fatal illness for infants.[32]

Finally, we come to obesity. Industrial farming has also resulted in the high sugar and fat, meat-rich and processed food diets which have triggered a worldwide obesity epidemic. When I had the pleasure of working with Jamie Oliver, as chair of the Jamie Oliver Food Foundation, he made a film in the US in which he encountered four generations of the same family, none of whom had ever cooked for their children, raising them on a diet of fast food and sugar-laden, ultra-processed foods instead. He also visited an elementary school in Huntington, West Virginia – then 'the unhealthiest city in America' – where the kids were served pizza at breakfast, and one child couldn't identify a bunch of fresh tomatoes.[33]

While these are admittedly extreme examples, they are also the logical endpoint of the remorseless drive for the production of cheap, empty calories (i.e. from added sugar and solid fats). Between 1975 and 2016, obesity trebled worldwide. By the end of that four-decade stretch, 1.9 billion adults were categorized as overweight, of whom 650 million were obese. Even more shockingly, in 2019, 38 million children under the age of five were considered overweight or obese.[34]

'We've reached a dead end'

Although we already produce enough cheap, empty calories to feed 10 billion today,[35] industrialized agriculture fundamentally undermines human, animal, plant and soil health. It has already proven calamitous for the environment and is adding fuel to the fire of climate change. The only way to limit and ultimately end the disastrous consequences I have listed – as well as feed humanity safely and sustainably – is for the world to pivot away from intensive agriculture and embrace measurable regenerative agriculture.

Let me say from the outset that I'm not advocating a return to the agricultural dark ages; rather, I believe we must harness both technology and bioscience, as well as the most important lessons farmers have learned along the way. Since the pre-industrial era, much of the world opted to venture down a very narrow agricultural path, where we progressively selected fewer and fewer crops (especially grains) with which to produce food, in large part due to limitations in science/technology (such as genetics) and techniques (the tools farmers had available to them).

Following the industrial revolution and particularly post-war, this blunt-instrument, monocrop approach to agriculture was only amplified, entrenched and rolled out worldwide, with the fallouts I've described so far in this chapter. Indeed, according to the FAO of the UN, 'Of the 250,000 to 300,000 known edible plant species, only 150–200 are used by humans. Only three – rice, maize and wheat – contribute nearly 60% of the calories and proteins obtained by humans from plants.'[36] In other words, we've reached an impasse; a dead end.

So what am I proposing we do next? Above all, we must be wary of, and resist, oversimplification, gimmicky solutions and

shortcuts, however superficially attractive they may seem.
In the last few years, for example, calls for people to shift
away from eating meat, primarily beef, to a plant-based
diet have grown to a clamour (amid a wider context where
consumption of meat is increasing globally[37]). Yet, as we saw
in Chapter 2, veggie burgers produced from industrially grown
monocrops (soya, peas, etc.) will also have a devastating
impact on the environment and local populations. And as
we'll see in Chapter 9, laboratory-grown or cultured meats are
not a good answer either. To my mind, they are yet another
iteration of 'fast food'.

Meanwhile, the marketing materials of venture-backed
companies like Impossible Foods and Beyond Meat make
much of their sustainability credentials, but arguably their claims
do not stand up to scrutiny (and it's worth pointing out that
one of the most widely cited supportive 'reports' favourably
comparing Beyond Meat's environmental impact with that of
a typical mass-produced beef burger turned out to have been
commissioned by Beyond Meat itself[38]).

Clearly, prioritizing plant-based burgers over beef or chicken
will dramatically reduce animal suffering. Similarly vegan
burgers, vegan sausages and the like will amount to a big
win for the environment once the impact of the entire supply
chain is considered to ensure healthiness for consumers and
sustainability for the growers of their ingredients. But we're
certainly not there yet. Today these much-hyped foods are also
based on monocrops, and according to Marco Springmann, a
senior environmental researcher from the University of Oxford,
suggestions that switching to Impossible/Beyond Meat burgers is
the most climate-friendly thing to do may be 'a false promise'.
He told NBC News that '... while their processed products have

about half the carbon footprint that chicken does, they also have five times more of a footprint than a bean patty'.[39]

As for whether they are healthier for us right now, once again the news is mixed. A study from Harvard Health found that while today's hyped meatless burgers are a good source of protein, vitamins and minerals, they are heavily processed, laden with large amounts of dubious flavourings and bindings, and high in saturated fat.[40]

Animal farming: 'It's not the cow, it's the how'

Similarly, while the replacement of animal proteins with plant-based products certainly has an important role to play, and there's no doubt that industrialized feed-based meat production is terrible for the planet, it's also true that livestock farming, and cows in particular, have had something of a bad press. Arguments often deployed against ruminants are that they damage the environment and/or contribute to climate change in three ways: a) they take up too much land; b) they require too much water; c) they produce and emit too much methane. All of those are both true and gross oversimplifications, and the conclusions are easily disproven.

Indeed, while too many intensively farmed cows are harmful for the planet, too few cows would be a problem, too. Unlike feed-based farming, 'intensive rotational grazing' – where livestock are regularly rotated onto new pastures, with the grazed grass then rested, allowing the urine and dung left behind to be processed by the microbes in the soil – improves the quality of the grass and restores plant biodiversity in degraded landscapes.

According to research from the University of Louisiana, Lafayette, cited in Gary Kleppel's *The Emergent Agriculture*,[41] the method also 'consistently resulted in lower methane emissions' and helps remove more carbon from the atmosphere. This practice stretches back over 10,000 years. Before cows were developed as farm animals (in south-east Turkey), their ancestors, the aurochs, and their cousins, the buffalos, roamed the vast prairies of Europe, Russia and North America. And going back even further, they shared those prairies with woolly rhinos and mammoths that were driven to extinction by our own Neolithic ancestors, unlike their African and Asian cousins that (barely) survived until the twenty-first century.

Without those meandering hooved herbivores, the prairies would not have survived as a thriving ecosystem. Small-scale, herb-grazing herds of cows provide the same vital function today. Most of the water they consume goes back into the soil, while their grazing and trampling of the soil provides the maintenance it needs to keep it healthy.

Impact creation tends not to be a linear process – in this case the impact of grazing mammals on land increases with the density of animals per given area, until it reaches an optimal point before it starts decreasing again. The art of regenerative farming is to reach and remain around that optimal point to deliver maximum impact.

Crop farming: 'Life in the soil thrives on variety'

A return to basics around crop rotation – perfected over thousands of years – would hold similar benefits for arable farming. As the Rodale Institute, an organic-farming focused non-profit, succinctly explains: 'Different plants have different nutritional needs and are susceptible to different pathogens and pests. If a farmer plants the exact same crop in the same place every year, as is common in conventional farming, they continually draw the same nutrients out of the soil. Pests and diseases happily make themselves a permanent home as their preferred food source is guaranteed. With monocultures like these, increasing levels of chemical fertilizers and pesticides become necessary to keep yields high while keeping bugs and disease at bay. Crop rotation helps return nutrients to the soil without synthetic inputs.'[42]

Why waste precious time and resources with crop rotation when additives could do it efficiently? It actually took until the beginning of the twenty-first century to fully grasp the nature of undersoil microbial activity, largely because it is anaerobic and the microorganisms die when they get exposed to oxygen in the air, so we could never observe their existence under our microscopes, nor would they reproduce in scientists' Petri dishes.

Recent biological breakthroughs improved our understanding of the complexity of soil microbiome that is so essential for the healthy development of plant and animal life.[43] However, our appreciation of this rich and productive underground life – beyond the earthworms tunnelling the soil, the micro arachnids and the microscopic anaerobic bacteria – that creates and maintains the ecosystem which enables plant roots and underground mycelium to work together, allowing plants to absorb the minerals and micronutrients that make our food rich in the nutrients we need, is still limited.[44]

The good news is that technology in the shape of big data, machine learning and genetics is already riding to the rescue. The Flanders Institute for Biotechnology, VIB – a leading 'entrepreneurial non-profit research institute', focused on the life sciences, based in Flanders, Belgium – has developed an ecosystem of agro-biotechnology start-ups and R&D units dedicated to plant technology.[45] One project, which began in 2021 and will take two years to complete, is investigating how to grow soybeans sustainably at scale locally in Flanders to end reliance on South American imports and reduce deforestation.[46] Among other things it aims to build a large collection of nitrogen-fixing bacteria and generate data that will improve the applicability of these bacteria for farming soy in Flanders.

Another example is Mineral, a computational agriculture project underway at X, Google's moonshot division.[47] According to the World Economic Forum, scientists estimate that of the 400,000 plants species on Earth, of which around half are edible for humans, we restrict ourselves to about two hundred species – just 0.1 per cent of the total.[48] The Mineral team argue that intensively growing a very limited variety of plants leaves our food supply vulnerable to pests, disease and a changing climate. 'Over time, it also depletes the soil of nutrients and minerals, reduces the diversity of the soil's microbiome, and diminishes the soil's ability to store carbon.' The net effect is a 'vicious cycle that makes our farmlands less productive and our food less nutritious'.

Still at the developmental stage at the time of writing, the project sets out to use new technology to harness nature's complexities rather than whittling it down to a few options. If plant breeders can unlock the genetic diversity of the tens of thousands of edible plants species we currently don't eat, they might be able to identify more resilient varieties that are better suited to our needs. 'If growers could understand how each and every plant on their farm is growing and interacting with its environment, they could reduce the use of fertilizer, chemicals and precious resources like water and explore sophisticated growing techniques like intercropping and cover cropping that restore soil fertility and increase productivity,' say Mineral's founders, outlining the scope of their mission.

To date the team have built software and hardware tools to gather data on environmental conditions in crop fields, such as soil, weather and historical crop data. They then developed a prototype plant buggy that moves through fields gathering high-quality images of each plant, mapping and classifying them down to the level of individual berries and beans.

Combining imagery compiled by the buggy with other data sets like satellite imagery, weather and soil information, the start-up is able to build a full and detailed picture of what's happening in the field and use machine learning to identify patterns and useful insights into how plants grow and interact with their environment. Thus equipped, plant breeders can then operate with full visibility, and accurately predict not only how different varieties of plants are likely to respond to a given environment, but also the size and yield of their crop. The data also means they can treat individual plants rather than, for example, having to spray entire fields.

This last point is especially salient when you consider the inaccuracy of current pesticide application. Today farmers typically soak their fields in pesticides – on which around $60 billion is spent annually – using very large nozzles on their sprayers, which in turn release large droplets. When the spray then hits the crop or weed, because of their size the droplets tend to bounce or slip off and end up in the ground, and from there the chemicals seep into the rivers through run-off and can ultimately end up in drinking water. It's estimated that around

70–80 per cent of pesticides do not reach their intended target, with about 50 per cent drifting away in the air onto neighbouring fields or land. The cumulative impact of this over years and decades is plainly environmentally catastrophic.

Dublin-headquartered MagGrow,[49] an Astanor portfolio company, has developed a patented proprietary technology that significantly slashes the waste associated with conventional pesticide spray applications. By using magnetic inserts to produce a positive and negative charge as the pesticide comes out of the sprayer, the farmer can optimize the flow of the liquid and significantly shrink the size of the droplets, with far more of them sticking to their target as a result of the magnetic charge. This innovation immediately reduces the volume of pesticides used by up to 30–40 per cent, depending on factors such as location and weather. The product, which is simply a boom that can be retrofitted onto the main body of an existing sprayer, also reduces the hazy mist associated with pesticide spraying, thereby diminishing the contamination of neighbouring crops and land.

While the hardware requires a fairly large initial outlay from the farmer – each unit costs in the region of €30,000 – MagGrow's technology delivers 20-per-cent increased coverage and up to 70 per cent drift reduction.[50] It also reduces costly chemical inputs by 25-per-cent and water usage by 50 per cent, extending spray windows and reducing labour. Indeed, the investment is amortized from the input savings alone in less than two years.

The EU's Farm to Fork Strategy has a target of reducing pesticide usage by 50 per cent by 2030. Individual countries such as Germany and the Netherlands have their own even more ambitious goals. Alongside other solutions such as bio-fertilizers, MagGrow's technology can help us get there and be a key driver in the transition to regenerative agriculture.

Rather than attempting to override or tame nature, the technological advances I've described, and many others besides, are for the most part exploiting its power, aikido-style, for good. They are learning from and working with it to accelerate processes such as plant breeding, genetic modification and crop discovery (or rediscovery), which might otherwise have taken scores or even hundreds of years, or, like MagGrow's technology, finding ways to minimize negative impacts. This path can allow us to wind down industrial agriculture with its diminishing returns and enable humanity to farm more sustainably and ultimately feed more people, more reliably, while steadily improving human health outcomes.

Waste not, want not
From toxic rivers to compostable shoes

In the engraving *Village Fair at Hoboken* (*c*.1559), attributed to Franz Hogenberg after Pieter Bruegel the Elder (see Figure 2, overleaf),[1] pigs and piglets are depicted foraging for food scraps as they weave among villagers enjoying the fair. Such intermingling, between hogs and humanity, was once the norm. As Europe's forests were cut down for firewood, and to make space for crops, wild pigs moved into towns and villages, where they roamed freely, scavenging for organic matter including human waste (in every sense), as well as the occasional corpse.

It is thought the modern pig's ancestors first appeared among humans some 10,000 years ago, when hunter-gatherers in Anatolia (Turkey) first settled in villages. Soon afterwards, the Eurasian wild boar moved into town to devour any leftovers – such as spoiled grain and rotten fruit – they could find. Over time those wild boar eventually became the domesticated pigs we know today.[2]

Pigs excelled not only at disposing of waste, but at generating very little of it themselves (once slaughtered). To this day almost the entire pig's carcass is recycled, from the parts

Figure 2

that are eaten (pork chops, ribs, etc.) to the sections that are processed into medicines, such as anticoagulants (blood thinners), and the bones, fat, skull and skin, which are 'super-cooked' at high temperatures (270°C) to produce pet food, livestock feed and biofuels.

The ancient Romans, too, famously wasted no part of the pig. According to the historian Mark Essig, author of *Lesser Beasts: A Snout-to-Tail history of the Humble Pig*:[3] 'No one loved pork the way the Romans loved pork. There's one surviving collection of recipes from the period. In it you'll find a few recipes for beef, you'll find maybe a dozen recipes for lamb, but there are dozens and dozens of recipes for pork; 17 recipes for suckling pig alone. And they really did use just about every part of the pig. They were (even) fans of devouring the womb.'

With their dependence on the whims of nature (drought, pests and floods) for their harvest and grain supply, alongside the ever-present threat of political turmoil, the Romans were frequently beset by famine. In 436 BC thousands of Romans drowned themselves in the Tiber rather than face death by starvation,[4] and between 123 and 250 BC the city of Rome was hit by famine one in every five years.[5] As a result of living at a time of such food precariousness, the urban poor in particular wasted no part of a slaughtered animal, even consuming 'the less desirable parts in blood puddings, regional sausages (*falisci, lucanicae*), meatballs (*isicia*), or stews at food stalls and taverns'.[6]

Modern life has made us wasteful

In our era of plenty, almost the complete reverse is true. Not only are we eating too much of certain things, which has led to surging obesity, but we are losing and/or wasting around a third of all the food produced for human consumption globally, which totals around 1.3 billion tons a year.[7]

According to the UNEP,[8] nearly half of all fruit and vegetables produced globally are wasted. The total cost of food losses and waste amounts to about $680 billion in industrial countries and $310 billion in developing countries. And, continues the UNEP, 'Every year consumers in rich countries waste almost as much food (222 million tons) as the entire net food production of sub-Saharan Africa (230 million tons).'

Moreover, we are seeing waste at every point of the production lifecycle from the farm, when it is spoiled or fails to conform to retailer/supermarket/ consumer expectations – typically misshapen or discolored vegetables – to restaurants, retailers and other food businesses and consumers, who overbuy and discard edible food that is unused, left over or passes (often arbitrary) 'best before' or 'use by' expiration dates.

Indeed, we consumers generate much of the waste in the system. It's our (unreasonable) expectations to see cheap, plentiful, fresh food, near-unlimited choice and constantly replenished supermarket aisles – in my experience, French supermarket customers panic when they don't see all thirty or so varieties of yoghurt on display! – that drives wasteful behaviour among producers, adds to the demand for volume and results in a far wider range of products than most people are ever likely to purchase in a lifetime.

When looked at from an impact point of view, where the full cost of food loss and waste is taken into account, the picture deteriorates further. The world-first Food Wastage Footprint (FWF) presented to the UN incorporated impacts on the atmosphere, water, land and biodiversity, and then translated these into societal costs, measured in monetary terms. It then developed a full-cost accounting (FCA) model 'to evaluate the direct financial costs, the lost value of ecosystems goods and services, and the loss of well-being associated with natural resource degradation'. Once all this was taken into account, the full costs of food waste rose from just under a trillion dollars to $2.6 trillion a year, including $700 billion of environmental costs and $900 billion of social costs.[9] To put that in perspective, that is almost the annual GDP of the UK ($2.8 trillion), currently the world's fifth largest economy.[10]

Plastics

There's another dimension to waste, too, which I have already touched on in Chapter 4: so-called 'single-use' plastics. As well as their impact on emissions, single-use plastic items such as containers and packaging, which constitute 40 per cent of plastics produced worldwide, are clogging the world's waterways and asphyxiating our oceans.[11] This is a problem that has worsened exponentially. Nearly half of all plastics ever manufactured were made in the last fifteen years, with production rising from 2.3 million tons in 1950 to 448 million in 2015, according to *National Geographic*. On current trajectories, plastics production is predicted to double by 2050. Moreover, the chemicals added to plastics to make them stronger, more flexible and durable mean that they can take up to 400 years to break down should they become litter.

And nearly all plastic does become litter: figures published by the UN in 2019 reveal that only 9 per cent of all plastic waste produced so far has ever been recycled. About 12 per cent has been incinerated, while the rest – 79 per cent – has ended up in landfills, dumps or the natural environment.[12] The impact of all this on the planet is as devastating, in its way, as GHG emissions and food waste, destroying natural habitats, carrying pollutants and harming wildlife – particularly all forms of aquatic life, ranging from whales to shrimp, mussels and oysters (thus entering the human food chain). Meanwhile, the micro-plastics and micro-fibres that result from plastic products broken down by the elements are found everywhere from the Himalayas to the depths of the oceans, according to the UNEP. They are in the air we breathe, the tap water we drink and even sewage systems, which are often clogged by plastic waste (particularly plastic bags), which can increase the transmission of vector-borne diseases like malaria.

And yet despite all of the above (and I'll come on to solutions later in the chapter), once again we should be wary of oversimplification and drastic solutions.

When looked at through the more exacting lens of an impact investor, a rather more nuanced picture of plastics emerges. In her memorable and engaging 2019 TEDx talk entitled 'Plastics Rehab',[13] Maastricht University's Kim Ragaert (formerly at Ghent), a leading authority on 'Circular Plastics', argues that when you step back from the public outrage, even hysteria, that plastic waste inspires and consider the facts dispassionately, actually 'plastics are functional and precious resources, which we need to keep in the materials loop'. Using a full life cycle analysis, Ragaert makes the point that a few grams of plastic wrapping extend the shelf life of cucumbers by eleven days and a steak by up to twenty-six, thereby minimizing food waste and resulting CO_2 emissions.

In fact, when scientists make an objective comparison between plastic and, say, glass and paper alternatives – by taking into account not only the materials a product requires, but also the land, water and energy used, plus the effects on human health, the ozone layer, land and water – plastics substantially outperform both from an impact point of view. Staggeringly, according to a life cycle assessment of plastic carrier bags by the UK's Environment Agency,[14] part of the government, when the full impact on the environment of making a reusable cotton shopping bag is taken into account, it would need to be used 173 times before being more environmentally friendly than a typical plastic bag (largely due to the chemicals and water required to grow cotton – a point I'll come on to shortly).

The real problem with plastics and the environment, says Ragaert, is the way we use and discard it; indeed, 80 per cent of the littering of plastic is intentional and caused by individuals rather than corporations. Which is why measurement and full impact analysis is so vital and innovators need to focus as much on the consumer-driven circular economy for plastics as on what comes next.

Fast fashion

Among consumer-facing industries, the fashion industry, and especially so-called 'fast fashion', has a particularly pernicious impact on the environment. In America alone 10.5 million tons of used clothing goes into landfill annually.[15] In fact, it is reckoned to be the second-worst polluter in the world after the oil industry.[16] In those countries where textiles are largely produced, untreated toxic wastewaters containing hazardous and carcinogenic chemicals are frequently dumped directly into rivers, damaging aquatic life and the health and livelihoods of the millions dependent on rivers, which in turn then carry that pollution into the world's oceans. Similarly, the use of fertilizers for cotton production is another source of water contamination, which heavily pollutes run-off waters.[17]

Second, fashion puts an enormous strain on freshwater supply, not only for the dyeing and finishing process for clothes (it can take 200 tons of freshwater per ton of dyed fabric), but also for the growth of cotton itself – up to 20,000 litres of water are required to produce a single kilo of cotton.[18] Third, every time a garment is washed it has been calculated that around 1,900 individual micro-fibres are released into the wastewater,[19] which are then found in the oceans and ingested by small aquatic organisms, which are later consumed by the fish we eat.

Other fallout from fast fashion includes the synthetic fibres, which take up to 200 years to biodegrade,[20] the chemicals used in cotton-growing (causing premature death among cotton farmers, along with freshwater and soil degradation) and fibres production, dyeing, bleaching and wet processing of garments, and greenhouse gas emissions (the apparel industry accounts for 10 per cent of global GHG emissions[21]).

Towards zero waste

The tsunami of waste generated by our throwaway consumer society – whether food, plastics, clothing or other disposable consumer goods – is in many ways the flipside of the coin to intensive agriculture. Both exact a grievous toll on Earth's balance sheet, with their full impact rarely, if ever, taken into account. Both require urgent remedial action.

However, across the board, innovators backed by impact funds are making significant, if incremental, inroads into the crisis I've described. Let's begin with food waste. Today food in most developed nations is cheap by historical standards. That's largely because the true cost of food is hidden from consumers. Researchers in Germany found that consumer prices would be far higher if the social and ecological impact of production were factored in (through true cost accounting).[22] Looking at four different indicators – land use change, greenhouse gas emissions, reactive nitrogen and the energy required for production – the report's authors found that if impact was fully accounted for, the price for minced meat, for example, would cost about three times as much as it does today, while Gouda cheese and milk would cost nearly twice as much.

Low prices also have a perverse incentive on consumption, encouraging a vicious cycle of intensive agricultural production with all the problems that entails, further stimulating consumption – and so on. If the full cost of production and impact were reflected in price, then organic food and food from regenerative farming would actually be cheaper than the industrialized variety (although it is more expensive today).

Cut-price food has another, more insidious effect on waste, too, namely that when food costs them so little (and, for example, in Europe in 2018, Britons spent just 7.8 per cent of their total household budget on food and non-alcoholic drinks – the least in Europe – while the Irish spent 8.7 per cent, Austrians 9.7 per cent, Germans 10.8 per cent, the French 13.1 per cent and Italians 14.1 per cent[23]) they don't mind throwing it away. They are also likely to spend less time planning meals to minimize waste, and err on the side of caution when it comes to 'expiry' labels such as 'sell by', 'best before' and 'use by' dates.

While food waste has fallen slightly in the UK – by 7 per cent or 480,000 tons between 2015 and 2018, according to British non-profit Waste Resources Action Programme (WRAP)[24] – households are still discarding 4.5 million tons of edible food, worth £14 billion a year (£700 a year for an average family). WRAP equates this with around 10 billion meals.

OLIO, a UK start-up (and a personal investment of mine), was set up to address this problem.[25] Co-founder Tessa Clarke says growing up on a dairy farm in North Yorkshire gave her a keen appreciation of the value of food. 'Many people probably don't have that anymore, because they're very disconnected from the origin of food. They're disconnected from how much hard work goes into it,' she says. 'Working on a farm meant that I grew up with a pathological hatred of food waste.'

Fast-forward to 2014, when Clarke was packing up to move back to the UK from Switzerland with her young family, and was left with a small amount of perishable food (specifically, sweet potatoes, cabbage and yoghurt) that she couldn't take with her. 'So I went out to try and find someone nearby to give it to,' she says. But the person she had in mind wasn't in her usual place outside the local supermarket on that particular day, and the prospect of knocking on multiple strangers' doors offering free food just seemed 'too weird'.

'And I hadn't got time for that anyway,' she recalls. 'It would have been really inefficient, as well as awkward and embarrassing.' Having worked in the digital space for over a decade by that point, Clarke says it just seemed intuitive to her that technology should have been able to easily connect her to neighbours to solve this problem. But no such app yet existed.

Back in the UK, when another digital start-up idea she'd been working on with OLIO's co-founder, Saasha Celestial-One (so-named by her Iowan 'hippy entrepreneur parents'), also focused on waste, didn't get off the ground, her mind returned to the experience of having to throw perfectly good food away for want of someone to share it with. Soon the idea that would become OLIO had begun to take shape.

Initial desk research revealed the scale of the food waste problem, while market research showed that it was an issue enough people cared deeply about. 'We got over 380 responses to our market research survey,' says Clarke. 'And the key insight was that one in three people agreed with the description that they were "physically pained" by throwing away good food. But just because it was a problem people cared about, didn't mean that they'd take the next step in our hypothesis, which was to share food with strangers. So before sinking our life savings into building an app, we decided to put it to the test.

'We came up with this idea of creating a WhatsApp group consisting of twelve people (from the survey) who all lived near each other – but didn't know each other, and didn't know us – who'd all said they were physically pained by throwing away good food. We decided to run the experiment for two weeks. We waited with bated breath for the first share, which took between twenty-four and forty-eight hours, and then there was quite a bit of sharing for the rest of the (trial). We then met with everyone face to face afterwards, separately, and there were three loud messages for us. One, we absolutely had to do this. Two, it only needed to be slightly better than a WhatsApp group. And then three – "How can I help?"'

'We were staring down the barrel of a food-sharing app with no food on it ...'

As they set to work Clarke and Celestial-One soon ran into a roadblock: early adopters who believed in the mission, by definition, hate food waste and therefore they didn't have any surplus food to upload to the app. 'We'd also somewhat naively hoped that local businesses such as cafés, bakeries and delis would use the OLIO app themselves, to bring footfall into their store, which would then drive increased brand awareness and they'd be able to cross-sell and up-sell and so on, but we quickly found that they didn't have the time to be messing about with an app. So we were staring down the barrel of a food-sharing app with no food on it, which is obviously highly concerning.'

Clarke continues: 'And then we realized what we needed to do was take our early adopters, who have time but no food waste, and match them with the businesses who have no time and loads of food waste. And that eventually became our (volunteer) Food Waste Heroes programme. We've now got over 40,000 trained volunteers, who we're recruiting on a daily basis from our community. We train them online on our proprietary food safety management system. We match them with their local business – they claim a collection slot, and then on their allotted time, they pick up all the unsold food from that business, take it home, take photos of it and add it to the app. Within minutes, their neighbors are requesting it. Minutes later, they're popping around to pick it up.'

OLIO's Food Waste Heroes programme has been key to the start-up's scaling, Clarke explains. 'One, it kickstarts supply, and supply then triggers notifications, which then brings people into the app. We've also found that people who have picked up free food from a Food Waste Hero are three times more likely to then go on and add their own. So it brings direct supply and also then indirectly brings more supply in. It results in virality and word of mouth – word spreads pretty quickly that there's free, say, Tesco food on the OLIO app. And then, of course, and absolutely critically, it has enabled us to develop a very robust, scalable and fast-growing revenue stream. So at the moment, those businesses are paying a waste contractor to take that surplus food off to landfill and instead they are now paying us to ensure that food is eaten in multiple homes in the local community.'

Today the company is making a significant dent in the blight of food waste. At the time of writing, 5 million people in sixty countries are on OLIO's free sharing app. Cumulatively they've shared over 34.3 million portions of food – saving the equivalent of 101 million car miles.[26] The team now also has partnerships with leading UK supermarket, retail and catering brands such as Tesco, Pret a Manger, Costa, Selfridges, Booker and Compass Catering to redistribute surplus food.

OLIO is just one of a number of mission-driven start-ups in this increasingly crowded field. Others include two Swedish apps: WhyWaste,[27] which works with supermarkets to reduce operational food waste, and Karma,[28] which is aiming to spark a movement it describes as 'radical slacktivism' by offering discounted food from 20,000-plus cafés and restaurants in Sweden and London. For businesses it provides a platform that allows them to sell both surplus food and food from their regular menu, while also feeding back data to help them ensure better production planning and reduce waste.

Too Good To Go,[29] meanwhile, is an app that also enables users to purchase surplus food cheaply from restaurants, bakeries, supermarkets and hotels, and now operates in seventeen countries. Not only is its model a win-win for the individual business – which can reach new customers and recover sunk costs – and the budget-minded consumer, but it also has a measurable impact on the planet. At the time of writing, the Copenhagen-based certified B Corporation start-up calculate they have saved over 104 million meals since 2016, thanks to almost 50 million users. Furthermore, the company is active in the public affairs space, too, seeking to influence governments in ripe-for-reform areas such as food expiry dates, which are estimated to be responsible for some 10 per cent of the 88 million tons of food waste across Europe (worth some €3–6 billion).[30]

San Francisco-born Afresh[31] is tackling fresh food waste from an enterprise resource planning standpoint, with AI-powered software that offers auto-generated predictions of demand and manages ordering, forecasting and store operations for grocery retailers across the US. Already used by grocers to order billions of pounds of food every year, at the time of writing the start-up claimed to have eliminated 6.9 million pounds of food waste, reduced 3.82 thousand tons of GHG emissions and saved 140 million gallons of water.

Meanwhile, Seattle-based Shelf Engine[32] has raised $41 million to date to reduce chronic in-store food waste (in the US, an estimated 40 per cent of deli sandwiches are wasted, 35 per cent of bread goes unsold and 14 per cent of fresh juice spoils) by fixing the grocery supply chain through automation. With mega-retailers such as Kroger and Walmart among its customers, the start-up's 'intelligent forecasting' system uses machine learning and probabilistic models – which are fed by 'vector autoregressive multivariate time series models that use a massive array of data sets' – to accurately predict demand, minimize waste and boost retailers' bottom line.

Another Astanor-backed firm, Apeel,[33] is reducing food waste and the need for plastic packaging by using 'cutin',[34] a material found in the peel, seeds and pulp of fruit and vegetables, to act as a protective 'second peel'. Part of the 'cuticle' which plays an important role in controlling water loss/transpiration and protecting produce from pests, cutin creates an extra layer thereby extending shelf life for produce by up to 100 per cent. Founded in 2012 with a grant from the Bill and Melinda Gates Foundation, Apeel – whose investors also include celebrities like Oprah Winfrey and Katy Perry – estimate that between the start of 2019 and August 2021 its plant-derived coating has saved over 42 million pieces of produce from going to waste at retail stores[35] (and this doesn't include produce saved in the home). The reason we, and others, have invested is the extraordinary system-wide impact of Apeel's technology. Specifically: fewer resources are wasted producing uneaten food, less plastic is required for packaging, less fuel for rapid shipping, less energy is expended on in-store refrigeration, fewer GHGs are emitted from wasted food in landfills and more people of all income levels have access to fresh fruit and vegetables.

The Californian start-up, which has raised over $640 million[36] since founding, uses life cycle analysis covering everything from raw materials used to waste disposal, to measure the holistic environmental impacts of incorporating its coating to extend the shelf life of fresh fruit and vegetables into the supply chains for avocados, limes, apples, mandarins and oranges. Looking at avocados alone, the LCA results show that Apeel avocados result in a 42 gram reduction in GHG emissions and require 14 litres less water per unit than standard avocados.[37]

As for fast fashion and plastics, I have already written (in Chapter 4) about Modern Meadow challenging the global leather industry and the use of animal collagen in cosmetics and healthcare products, and NotPla, which is bidding to end single-use plastic wrapping and containers. Rival Xampla,[38] a Cambridge University spin-off, is also working on reducing plastic waste, but in their case with a plant protein material alternative to plastic sachets, flexible packaging films and micro-plastics within liquids and lotions.

And there are many other impact-driven businesses in the space, vying for a slice of this rapidly expanding market. A few of these include Eindhoven-based Searious Business,[39] an impact-driven start-up that helps big business (including Nestlé, Danone, Heineken and Unilever) introduce circular plastic use in packaging, furniture and consumer electronics, the UK's WAES,[40] producers of the world's first plastic-free sustainable trainers (made with compostable natural rubber and carbon positive soles), and Calyxia,[41] a French company in the Astanor portfolio, which is aiming to replace plastic microencapsulation with more advanced and biodegradable microcapsules for the home, mobility and sustainable agriculture.

Each year, around 42,000 tons of non-biodegradable micro-plastics end up in the environment,[42] accumulating in animals, including fish and shellfish, and thus entering the human food chain. As European (EU) legislation moves progressively towards banning added micro-plastics and micro-beads in most products,[43] Calyxia microcapsules are the only capsules independently determined to be fully biodegradable according to the OECD (Organisation for Economic Co-operation and Development) 301 biodegradability test.[44] The Paris-headquartered company has been granted nine patents in its manufacturing process, with two more pending.

For too long, when it comes to waste the status quo has been tolerated simply because food and goods appear mostly cheap to produce, and their disposability has been good for margins (and an easy option for consumers). Only our rivers and oceans, the natural world and the poorest who directly depend on them have been living (and dying) with the consequences. Yet with the frenzy of innovation in the space, a tipping point – driven by rapidly shifting consumer expectations – may at last be approaching. Measuring every dollar invested in a company, and every decision that same company makes, for impact as well as profit, brings that day ever closer.

Gut instinct
Health, gut and germs

A decade ago, at the Future of Food Conference at Georgetown University, Washington DC, Prince Charles delivered a speech that was remarkable for its prescience.[1] Frequently mocked at home for his curious habit of talking to plants and shaking hands with trees,[2] the Prince of Wales was a champion of organic and regenerative farminglong before they went mainstream.[3] After calling for the attainment of a system where the production of healthier food was rewarded, becomes more affordable for consumers and doesn't take such a heavy toll on 'the Earth's capital', he said:

'Nobody wants food prices to go up, but if it is the case that the present low price of intensively produced food in developed countries is actually an illusion, only made possible by transferring the costs of cleaning up pollution or dealing with human health problems onto other agencies, then could correcting these anomalies result in a more beneficial arena where nobody is actually worse off in net terms? It would simply be a more honest form of accounting that may make it more desirable for producers to operate more sustainably ...'

Fallout from the global agri-food system has deteriorated further in the decade since that speech was delivered. As we've seen, dishonest accounting is still pervasive and propping up a production model that focuses on volume and quantity at the expense of quality, largely because of the lingering power of the reductionist, food-as-fuel approach I described in Chapter 6.

And the danger signs are flashing once more, suggesting that, rather than learning from our mistakes, if anything we are on the cusp of replacing the attitude captured in Fritz Kahn's illustration, which depicts the body 'as a chemical plant in which food is being broken down in the intestinal tract and processed through the liver to power the muscles', with a new version, only this time stamped 'Designed in Silicon Valley'.

'No time? No problem!'

If you are in any doubt that we are in danger of swapping one take on heavily processed 'fast food' (burgers, chicken nuggets, pizzas, waffles and Pop-Tarts) with another, then I'd suggest a quick scan of the Soylent website.[4] The venture-backed, Valley-born meal replacement brand – which garnered widespread publicity as a solution for time-poor tech bros who shared Elon Musk's disturbing, much-quoted philosophy,[5] 'If there was a way that I couldn't eat so I could work more, I would not eat …' – confronts visitors to its homepage with essentially the same time-saving 'food = units of energy' rationale as that depicted in Kahn's illustration:

'When there is no time, grab a Soylent and have a nutritious meal that is as easy as it is delicious!' it declares. And: 'We create products that deliver complete nutrition in convenient formats so you can get your fill anywhere, anytime ...'

Once memorably dismissed in *Fast Company* as 'basically SlimFast for men',[6] Soylent – which is now profitable – was in the process of reinventing itself through a concerted push into the major retailers such as Walmart at the time of writing, under the leadership of the new CEO who handily comes from both a plant-based milk and traditional Big Food background.[7] However, whether the start-up's 'complete drinkable meal' – or indeed the wares of any of the other leading meal replacement contenders such as Huel, Ample Foods or Jimmy Joy – will ever be more than niche remains to be seen; its claim 'to create products that deliver complete nutrition' raises far more questions than it answers when it comes to human health (I'll come on to why in a moment).

'No kill' meat

Of course, meal replacement shakes (and the like) are not the only show in town. An equally hyped science-driven solution to the crisis caused by intensive farming is lab-grown or cultured meat, a technology that has recently attracted feverish investor check-writing. Against a backdrop where the market for meat alternatives could be worth as much as $140 billion by 2029, according to Barclays Investment Bank research[8] – a generous 10 per cent slice of the global meat industry – (relatively early-stage) start-ups are, if not exactly flourishing, then certainly making incremental progress, as well as headlines.

Israeli start-up Future Meat Technologies, for example, recently announced that its lab-grown chicken is on track for price parity with genuine poultry,[9] an important milestone in a sector that has always been hampered by sky-high production costs. In December 2021, the company closed a $347 million funding round, the largest ever for a cultivated meat,[10] to build a US production facility. The Dutch food technology company Mosa Meat, based in Maastricht,[11] says that a single peppercorn-sized sample of the cells it harvests from cows, and then cultures to become muscle and fat, can eventually provide sufficient meat to produce 80,000 burgers.

Bill Gates-, Richard Branson- and SoftBank-backed UPSIDE Foods (formerly Memphis Meats) – producers of the world's first cultured beef meatball in 2016, which carried a $1,000 price tag at the time – said it was hoping to share its first cultivated meat products with consumers imminently.[12] In Singapore, meanwhile, at the tail end of 2020, San Francisco-born Eat Just, best known for its mung-bean-based egg alternative, won approval from the Singapore Food Agency (SFA) for its lab-grown chicken to be sold commercially, believed to be a regulatory world-first for cultured meat.[13] Another home-grown Singaporean start-up, Shiok Meats,[14] which is growing crustacean meat from muscle cells, 'plans to commercialize' in 2022. (Singapore is at the epicentre of lab-grown meats partly due to the technical expertise on the island city-state and deep specialism in stem cell research, but also because of the government's '30 by 30' policy for the country to produce 30 per cent of its nutritional needs by 2030, as a buffer against supply disruptions.)

These are just a handful of the early success stories in the field. However, once again, for all the obvious upsides for the environment, as well as removing the need to slaughter animals (or use antibiotics and growth hormones), claims made by proponents of this lab-grown version of processed food may not stand up to scrutiny, especially with regard to human health outcomes. In most, if not all, of the above examples of cultured meat start-ups, cells are sourced from an animal's fat or, more frequently, muscles. But whether the resulting tissue would offer much nutrition, which cannot be obtained from plants, let alone from a full animal, is at the very least open to question.

'What is very important is that we – and what I mean by "we" is complex organisms, what we call eukaryotes – live in symbiosis and (our) bacteria produce vectors (or molecules), metabolites and so on, that play a role also in our biology,' says Karine Clément, professor of nutrition at Pitié Salpêtrière Hospital and director of Nutriomics (Nutrition and Obesities: Systemic Approaches research unit) at Inserm and Sorbonne University in Paris. 'One consequence of this is that they also produce molecules that are helpful for our growth, development and immune maturation.'

'In that context, if you consider developing, say, a heart in the lab from progenitors – which are cell precursors – the heart will need (its) environment, as well as other tissues, organs and its nervous system and so on, to function. Similarly, if you grow meat from muscle cells in vitro, without the key environment including metabolites from the bacteria, I wonder whether the quality of the meat in this case would be equal to the meat from an (entire) animal fed properly.'

In other words, cultured in isolation from its environment, it is likely, probable even, that the lab-grown variety does not have anything like the same nutritional value for our gut as meat that derives from a whole animal, with its complex network of organs, fat reserves, nervous system and microbiome. And, of these, it is our microbiome – the genetic material of all the microbes, including bacteria, fungi, protozoa, yeast and viruses, that live on and inside the human body, mostly in our gut[15] – that is increasingly considered to be the most significant.

Gut instinct

The study of the human microbiome is still, strictly speaking, an emergent scientific area. As far back as the nineteenth century, scientists such as the chemist and microbiologist Louis Pasteur and Russian zoologist and immunologist Élie Metchnikoff had begun to explore the relationship between bacteria and human health. Progress, however, was severely constrained, mostly due to the fact that bacteria living in the human gut, and more particularly the colon, cannot survive in the presence of oxygen, which made cultivating them for laboratory research highly complex.

Following the sequencing of the human genome in 2003, however, it became possible to sequence bacteria from faecal material (without the need for oxygen). This precipitated a burst of scientific activity leading to a number of breakthroughs through the mid-2000s and beyond to the point where the human microbiome is now widely recognized as essential for human development, immunity and nutrition. According to the Center for Eco-genetics and Environmental Health at the University of Washington:[16] 'The bacteria in the microbiome help digest our food, regulate our immune system, protect against other bacteria that cause disease, and produce vitamins including B vitamins B12, thiamine and riboflavin, and Vitamin K, which is needed for blood coagulation.'

Today we know that autoimmune diseases such as MS, rheumatoid arthritis, muscular dystrophy and fibromyalgia have been associated with dysfunction in the microbiome.

Furthermore, researchers have discovered that our microbiome acts almost as 'a remote control' for other aspects of human health from how our metabolisms function to our brain health,[17] including by triggering mood swings, motivation and concentration loss.[18]

Yet it's the link between microbiome and obesity that is of particular relevance to this narrative. A 2008 study comparing the core gut microbiome in obese and lean twins found that obese participants had reduced bacterial diversity compared with those that were lean.[19] A second study some eight years later in the UK, published in *Genome Biology*, also found, among other things, that participants with less bacterial diversity in their gut had a higher proportion of visceral fat[20] (linked toincreased risk of type 2 diabetes and cardiovascular disease). [21]

Professor Karine Clément, who, among other duties, heads a research group working on the pathophysiology of obesity, says that while it has been shown repeatedly across multiple studies that people suffering from obesity and/or type 2 diabetes have 'lost diversity and richness of the gut microbiota', it is too early to infer causality, i.e. that changes in the gut microbiota play a definitive role in the development of these conditions in the first place.

'There was a recent statement from the European Commission which stated that obesity is a chronic condition, and I believe that the gut microbiota contribute to the maintenance of this chronic condition, because when you have decreased richness in the microbiome, this also contributes to metabolic changes. So, for example, resistance to insulin as well as low-grade inflammation, which is a very important component of some of these chronic diseases. Now the key challenge is to develop approaches targeting the gut microbiota – such as dietary approaches, or the use of pre-, pro- or post-biotics) to improve a subject's metabolism. We are working on that in my lab right now.'

The correlation between microbiome and obesity, meanwhile, was only reinforced during the pandemic, when researchers discovered that the variety and volume of gut microbiome may influence the severity of COVID-19, as well as the immune system's response to the disease.[22] Writing in the journal *Gut*, the team concluded: 'Associations between gut microbiota composition, levels of cytokines (cell signalling molecules that facilitate communication between cells in immune responses)[23] and inflammatory markers in patients with COVID-19 suggest that the gut microbiome is involved in the magnitude of COVID-19 severity possibly via modulating host immune responses.' Furthermore, their findings suggested that imbalances in the microbiome may also be implicated in 'persisting inflammatory symptoms', commonly known as long COVID.

All of which brings us back to diet and the impact of the global-intensive agri-food system, which has elevated the production and distribution of cheap calories over genuine nutrition. This combination of poor-quality food, consumed in vast amounts, has resulted in an epidemic of diet-related diseases, and in the process weakened the health of large swathes of the population – and frequently among societies' most deprived – leaving them vulnerable to opportunistic viruses such as COVID-19.

'We are eating DNA and RNA all the time'

In her article 'Eating as Dialogue, Food as Technology',[24] which I quoted from in Chapter 6, Hannah Landecker goes on to argue that greater understanding of the human microbiome and the role of the gut means that hundred-year-old 'food = fuel' notions about the link between food, eating and health have finally been sidelined. She writes:

'From the burgeoning science of the human microbiome to a sophisticated understanding of the human intestinal tract as a dense site of information exchange and sensory complexity, researchers are beginning to understand the complex conversation among foodstuffs, microbes and human cells and organs ... (They) are testing components of food, and the biochemical products that our metabolisms generate from food, as signals that could potentially be harnessed to tweak cellular energy use or tissue repair.'

This, Landecker continues, presents us with a fresh set of answers to the question: what is food?

'When we eat plants, animals and fungi, we are eating more than calories or carbohydrates, proteins, fats and vitamins. All organisms have their own cells and their own genomes. Therefore, we are eating DNA and RNA all the time. It has long been assumed that these materials are completely broken down and used as building blocks for the eater's needs. While this is certainly the case for most consumed molecules, there are other stories unfolding at the microscopic scale of cellular interaction in the intestinal tract.'

It is such stories that help explain why the path offered by meal replacements and lab-cultured meats is ultimately a blind alley. While they may offer the requisite protein, vitamins, essential nutrients and so on, this ultra-processed food ignores the complexity of the microbiome in our gut – and the role it plays in our health. One way to look at this Valley-inspired 'tech-solutionist' approach – which views food as just another problem to be 'solved' – is as the screening-out of risk and the 'dirty' side of nature. A corporate giant like Nestlé, for example, sets out to protect its customers from 'germs' across the human lifespan, from baby formula for the earliest days of infancy, to its nutrition solutions pitched at the elderly who may be suffering from age-associated cellular decline.[25] (Incidentally Nestlé also recently launched a powdered milk drink for senior citizens in China.[26]) However, this de-risked version of nature – 'Nature, only safer!' – that Silicon Valley has in store for us is not the antidote to the excesses of the current agri-food system, but an excessive swing of the pendulum to another extreme, where we've partially answered some questions (environmental footprint, perhaps), but flunked arguably the biggest issue of all: better long-term human health.

Healthy equilibrium

The idea that tech can, let alone should, protect us from nature is a red herring. Life *is* dangerous and the notion of being able to live 'risk-free' illusory. So we shouldn't be using technology to take us further away from nature – the soil, animals and plants, and the life within them – but to bring us closer to it instead. Above all to enable us to rediscover a healthy equilibrium between nature's dangers and benefits.

Scientists are still far from any conclusive understanding of the human microbiome and how it impacts upon our physical and mental health – for example, much research has yet to be done into areas such as how and whether our microbiome can be tinkered with to improve health outcomes, and how exactly the human host and microbe community interact. However, advances in this sphere make it all the more urgent to address the issue of why humanity has pursued a curative or reparative course when it comes to human health, rather than a preventative one.

Over the course of half a century, through a dysfunctional agri-food system, developed nations have collectively spent trillions of dollars addressing food and diet-related illnesses, a crisis humanity has engineered itself from scratch. Ultimately this has resulted in a double whammy where not only have we built a defective system at the expense of the environment, but on top of that we've directed all our resources towards trying to patch up the consequences rather than addressing the root cause. It's as if we're supplying a patient with bandages without ever asking them why they're repeatedly banging their head against a wall.

Looked at from an impact perspective, this makes no sense at all. Huge strides made in our knowledge of the microbiome and how it might soon be tweaked and targeted by the food we ingest to improve human health show why nothing short of a complete overhaul in our thinking is now essential. Rethought and systematically rebuilt, a new, regenerative, farming-led food system would assign, at the very least, equal priority to the food that we require for our energy as that we consume, to ensure equilibrium between our health, gut and 'germs'.

Impact investing is based on the premise that, rather than nudging companies towards improving their external effects by a degree or two here and there – often a form of greenwashing – we must alter their entire trajectories instead. The only way that can be achieved is through the faster adoption of properly resourced disruptive technologies, combined with the genuine alignment of purpose and measurable outcome.

In my current field of agri-tech impact investing I've come to see the microbiome as, in effect, my 'compass': specifically, if a particular process or product doesn't have a positive impact on the microbiome – from the microbes in the soil beneath our feet, to plants and animals, and ultimately the human gut – then it takes us in the wrong direction. Applied more broadly, all forms of investing, whether private or institutional, should be undertaken with an impact compass similarly in hand.

Yes, that's starting to happen. Amid ramped-up rhetoric and bandwagon-jumping, the last couple of years have seen a rebalancing towards ESG-focused investing, which is an important first step in the right direction. But incremental shifts are nowhere near enough. Within a few years, 'slightly better than the status quo' will see many of the UN's SDG goals (and their equivalents) slip beyond reach. Net zero will surely remain a pipe dream, too. Only radical change will suffice now, with these four headline priorities for the financial and business worlds: reform finance; fund innovation; align mission and outcome. And, always, measure for impact. Our planet's health, and our own, depend on us getting this right.

Coda
Five transitions for reconciling capitalism and ecology

'There will be no "Planet B" anytime soon'

Over the course of these pages I've attempted to set out
the broader context for the crisis the world faces today as it
continues to wrestle with the fallout from the global intensive
agri-food system and consider what needs to be done to
achieve real and lasting change. Of the many remedial
steps I've argued for – including for impact to become
the dominant model for investing globally, the widespread
adoption of alternative financial models including the triple
bottom line (TBL) and true cost accounting (TCA), alongside
the introduction of rigorous life cycle analysis (LCA), wherever
applicable – I believe there are five key societal and business
transitions we must make urgently to place humanity (back)
onto a sustainable path.

1. Introduce a new globally recognized accounting system

Over the next few years we need to bring about nothing short of a revolution in accounting and bookkeeping on a par with the adoption of the GAAP (generally accepted accounting principles) in the 1930s and 1940s to bring 'external' environmental and societal costs at the centre of everyday's attention of managers.

Just as GAAP was developed as a set of rules, essentially to standardize accounting practices for corporations and businesses, today we must make accounting for 'externalities' – including a very thorough life cycle analysis of impact on the environment and society – the bookkeeping baseline for organizations and businesses of all sizes. From global brands to brand new start-ups to the likes of national postal services and even elementary school budgets, bookkeeping needs to move away from the partial, siloed view that P&L accounts offer to become, in a sense, three-dimensional. As we've seen in Chapter 2, at COP26 held in Glasgow in November 2021, the IFRS Foundation announced the creation of the International Sustainability Standard Board (ISSB) with a mission to establish disclosure standards, which will insert climate, social and governance data into the price and cost of capital mechanisms and will allow capital allocations guided by these data. It will take a few years for these new accounting rules to be agreed upon and adopted by all. Until that happens, companies and organizations should not sit still because, in the meantime, it is nature that is paying for the unaccounted costs – and the worst affected are the most fragile human and animal populations.

An example of how changing accounting could already start in communities might be to look at a school's food purchasing budget. A school that offers mass-produced chicken nuggets or sugar-laced meatballs in tomato sauce to its children at lunchtime every day is almost certainly doing so for budgetary reasons. Serving freshly cooked chicken and noodles or fish with vegetables might cost 20 per cent more per head. Yet when you conduct an LCA, and factor in the cost that perhaps a quarter of these children will go on to develop diet-related diseases – and the enormous burden that places on those individuals and society over a lifetime – then skimping on school meals makes no sense at all for the community.

We cannot blame our predecessors for implementing this state of affairs, because plainly they did not possess the tools – the data, computing power, or indeed the internet itself – to do things differently. We have no such excuses today. Just as, say, Google has put together libraries of machine-learning systems, we will soon be able to rely on publicly available and transparent LCAs for everything from school meals to road repairs or building a new office block.

2. Pivot to an impact-inspired subsidies and tax incentive model

By fully integrating externalities into accounting and achieving radical transparency, governments and central (and retail) banks can more easily focus taxation on those who are deriving profits from negatively impactful activities. Responsible behaviour can then be incentivized, with subsidies (especially in the farming sector) offered to those who are producing a healthy triple bottom line.

The corollary of establishing a new model for accounting is that deploying governmental tools to drive behaviour change would become far easier and more transparent. In one of the largest such programmes in the world, for example, the EU currently lavishes some €59 billion ($65 billion) annually on Common Agricultural Policy (CAP) subsidies to Europe's farmers, much of which goes to upholding the current opaque, malfunctioning and often corrupt status quo,[1] while doing much to undermine the EU's own sustainability goals and ultimately its reputation with its own constituents. (The good news is that post-COVID, the European Commission has been working on a new CAPaligned to the Green Deal, with higher environmental and climate ambitions.[2] New objectives include mandatory redistribution of income support – member states will have to redistribute at least 10 per cent to the benefit of small farms. The new CAP will also fully integrate EU environmental and climate legislation: 'CAP Plans will contribute to the targets of the Farm to Fork and Biodiversity strategies, and will be updated to take into account the changes in the climate and environmental legislation from the European Green Deal.')

Far more must be done to allow governments, from supranational bodies to local authorities, to use levers such as subsidies and tax relief to incentivize climate-friendly practices, such as regenerative farming.[3] The ability to monitor and measure impact thanks to LCAs, alongside TBL accounting, also enables banks – central, business and retail – to issue bonds or lend against strict ESG/Green criteria, penalizing (through higher interest rates or by not lending to) those who have a negative impact on the environment, even if they are very profitable. By the same token, companies that are actively fixing environmental problems would be prioritized.

3. Develop environmental education programmes and transparency at scale

To foster change in consumption practices, we must empower citizens to make properly informed choices and reduce the real inequality of food education for the underprivileged. Armed with the requisite information, consumers could then insist on full supply chain transparency, especially for the food they buy or order at restaurants, or in supermarkets, and boycott those chains or products that do not meet the right standards.

Consumer-led change, powered by social media, is here to stay, but the full disclosure enabled by LCAs and TBL accounting promises to allow many more of us to make far better-informed choices about what we eat, wear and buy. Research for VIF (*Vivons en forme*),[4] a French non-profit that mobilizes local authorities/actors to support families to live healthier and more active lives, found that the chance of being overweight and/or obese was greatly exacerbated by socio-economics and education: 50 per cent of children who grow up in a household where no one has a higher education diploma consume sugary drinks every day. That number plummets to just 7 per cent in households that have achieved a Baccalaureate plus two or more years of further education.

Without raising awareness through programmes and training about the dangers of highly processed foods and the damage caused by intensive agriculture, progress will remain limited. Full, easily digestible LCAs at every consumer outlet – whether restaurant, supermarket or e-commerce platform – should be made available by law. Apps are already making it easier to shop by placing all the information we need at our fingertips. In Belgium and France Nutri Score's SmartWithFood app allows consumers to make better-informed shopping decisions by equipping them with full product transparency and personalized food recommendations, while offering participating retailers increased sales and loyalty.[5]

Widely used in France and Belgium, independent French app Yukadeciphers product labels and analyses the health impact of food products and cosmetics – also providing a detailed data sheet for each product to explain how it was evaluated.[6] Where a food item scores poorly, the app will recommend similar products that are better for a user's health (and will do so with true independence, as Yuka does not take a cut of the sale or a fee for the lead).

Some supermarkets are even further ahead of the curve. Colruyt, a chain headquartered in Halle, covering Belgium, France and Luxembourg, has introduced Eco-Score,[7] which takes into account the LCA of a product, across sixteen impact categories that 'play an important role from the creation to the disposal of a product', including climate change, water usage, land use, particulate matter, acidification and so on – a far more powerful approach than simply measuring CO_2 emissions or carbon footprint.

Meanwhile, in Chile OK to Shop enables users to view a product's full ingredients and certification from nutritionists and regulators.[8] Direct behaviour-changing intervention from the Chilean government has proven effective, too, with black-and-white food labelling warning of high sugar, salt or fat content carried on the front of unhealthy processed foods and sugary drinks. Consumption of sodas has been slashed by almost a quarter in Chile, where there is an obesity epidemic, since it was first introduced by the Ministry of Health[9]*

4. Ramp up support for new technology development

This revolution will be underpinned by the most innovative of new tech and big data, and it will only be through vastly increased investment and opening up public contracts to innovators that the shift to sustainable production – as well as helping nature regenerate, and rebuilding biodiversity – will be secured.

Beyond funding from impact investors, scientists and technologists need access to sustained and free-flowing capital if they are going to succeed in tackling many of the daunting global issues I have described in this book. Yes, in large part this is about increased access to public (impact) funding sources, but it's also about removing the obstacles to encourage governments and large corporations to buy from small, unproven and disruptive companies. Large organizations are risk-averse and often feel most comfortable when they're sitting across the table (or video screen) from similarly large players, and have a tendency to award the biggest contracts to the largest multinationals. That approach is obviously an innovation killer.

---

* Author's note: One last point. We know from behaviour during the pandemic that some people would not make the right choice even if they were armed with sufficient information; and pressure from social media campaigns will not ensure change that lasts longer than, say, an electoral cycle. That's why we must consider introducing ways to hold decision-makers (government ministers and senior company executives) accountable for the long-term consequences of their actions (or inaction).

The British government was a pioneer in this regard by opening up large government contracts to start-ups, and pledging to spend £1 in every £3 with small businesses (which it achieved by 2020).[10] Historically, the US approached this same issue very effectively by enabling Silicon Valley start-ups to compete for lucrative government defence contracts, during the Cold War and space race. (The US federal government was the key customer for early chip technology, for example.) In the 1970s, laws that removed restrictions on investing and capital gains tax paved the way for the venture capital industry, which has done so much to electrify the innovation economy.

Similar farsightedness and a stomach for risk-taking are required today, when we are relying on a new generation of disruptive players to build the technology that will power this revolution and achieve the scientific breakthroughs we need in regenerative farming, and to rebuild biodiversity. A new wave of impact investors will back these early-stage entrepreneurs, as they develop their technology and bring it to market. But we need wholesale legislative intervention to clear the way for governments at every level, and for large organizations and corporates to become clients far earlier in the start-up life cycle, instead of relying on incumbents who perpetuate the status quo instead.

There are some positive signs at the supranational level. One clear example is the European Commission's Sustainable Finance programme,[11] which will help deliver key objectives under the European Green Deal as well as meet the EU's international obligations on climate and sustainability. As part of its bid to 'reorient capital flows towards sustainable investment and market transparency', the Commission is also adopting 'an EU classification system for sustainable activities' (i.e. a legal framework or taxonomy). These – alongside initiatives to boost R&D and innovation, such as Horizon 2020,[12] which committed €80 billion worth of funding between 2014 and 2020 – are indicative of progress. But they need to dedicate far greater resources and financial firepower, much faster, given the urgency and gravity of the situation.

5. Get lobbying

Individual investors should lobby their banks, financial institutions, pension funds and financial advisors to opt out of investments that do not support a sustainable future for the inhabitants of this uniquely liveable planet. And lobby their local, regional and global leaders to act urgently. After all, there will be no 'Planet B' anytime soon.

Consumer-led impact investing is the final piece of the jigsaw. Individuals, especially when acting as an activist pack, wield tremendous power by pushing corporations to produce differently for them. The importance of lobbying for a more sustainable approach to agri-food production cannot be overstated, whether that's demanding radical transparency in farming practices and food nutrition or supporting the agricultural transition to sustainable farming by using alternative funding platforms such as MiiMOSA or LITA.[13,14] Individuals alone can take small steps by making everyday consumption choices that are good for their own health and good for the planet, improving their 'carbon or environmental footprint'. But then in turn by lobbying the leaders of their communities or their countries they activate something bigger as, once convinced by the arguments and the urgency of taking action at a local and global level, these leaders have access to much more powerful levers of transformation by both regulating and by altering the flow of taxes and subsidies. This is how everyone can improve their own 'carbon or environmental shadow' (or influence), making it an order of magnitude more impactful than their own footprint.

Sources

Introduction

1   Tom Huddleston Jr, 'Bill Gates was very surprised by crazy COVID conspiracy theories', CNBC, 01/27/2021, https://www.cnbc.com/2021/01/27/bill-gates-was-very-surprised-by-crazy-covid-conspiracy-theories.html

2   Milton Friedman, 'A Friedman doctrine …', *New York Times Magazine*, 13/09/1970, https://www.nytimes.com/1970/09/13/archives/a-friedman-doctrine-the-social-responsibility-of-business-is-to.html

3   Margaret Thatcher Foundation, 'Thatcher, Hayek & Friedman', https://www.margaretthatcher.org/archive/Hayek

4   Jon Vidal et al., 'Margaret Thatcher: her impact and legacy in global development', *Guardian*, 04/16/2013, https://www.theguardian.com/global-development/poverty-matters/2013/apr/16/margaret-thatcher-impact-legacy-development

5   'Statement on Corporate Governance', Business Roundtable, September 1997, https://cdn.theconversation.com/static_files/files/693/Statement_on_Corporate_Governance_Business-Roundtable-1997%281%29.pdf?1566830902

6   Tom Zeller Jr, 'Thousands march in Copenhagen calling for action', *New York Times*, 12/12/2009, https://www.nytimes.com/2009/12/13/science/earth/13climate.html

7   Lisa W. Foderaro, 'Taking a call for Climate Change to the streets', *New York Times*, 09/21/2014, https://www.nytimes.com/2014/09/22/nyregion/new-york-city-climate-change-march.html

8   John Cook, 'Ten years on: how Al Gore's *An Inconvenient Truth* made its mark', The Conversation, 05/30/2016, https://theconversation.com/ten-years-on-how-al-gores-an-inconvenient-truth-made-its-mark-59387

9   'Larry Fink's 2018 Letter to CEOs', BlackRock, https://www.blackrock.com/corporate/investor-relations/2018-larry-fink-ceo-letter

10   'Business Roundtable Redefines the Purpose of a Corporation', Business Roundtable, 08/19/2019, https://www.businessroundtable.org/business-roundtable-redefines-the-purpose-of-a-corporation-to-promote-an-economy-that-serves-all-americans

11   Robert Reich, 'The biggest business con of 2019 ...', *Guardian*, 12/29/2019, https://www.theguardian.com/commentisfree/2019/dec/29/boeing-amazon-business-ethics-robert-reich

12   Attracta Mooney, 'Climate change: asset managers join forces with the eco-warriors', *Financial Times*, 07/26/2020, https://www.ft.com/content/78167e0b-fdc5-461b-9d95-d8e068971364

13   Dianna Christie, 'Kantar: Consumers want brands to take stance on social issues ...', 06/11/2020, https://www.marketingdive.com/news/kantar-consumers-want-brands-to-take-stance-on-social-issues-but-demograp/579618/

14   https://fridaysforfuture.org/

15   https://www.who.int/news-room/fact-sheets/detail/obesity-and-overweight

16   'Hellmann's mayo switches to free-range eggs', *Poultry World*, 02/12/2008, https://www.poultryworld.net/Broilers/Markets--Trade/2008/2/Hellmanns-mayo-switches-to-free-range-eggs-WP002186W/

17   Hannah Richardson, 'Marcus Rashford welcomes school holiday support climbdown', BBC News, 11/08/2020, https://www.bbc.co.uk/news/education-54841316

18   https://www.fidelitycharitable.org/insights/2021-future-of-philanthropy/new-definition.html

19   Scott Shane, 'The Business of War: Google Employees Protest Work for the Pentagon', *New York Times*, 04/04/2018, https://www.

nytimes.com/2018/04/04/technology/google-letter-ceo-pentagon-project.html

20 Kate Clark, 'Protestors call on Salesforce to end contract with border patrol agency', TechCrunch, 09/25/2018, https://techcrunch.com/2018/09/25/protestors-call-on-salesforce-to-end-contract-with-border-patrol-agency/

21 Kari Paul, 'Hundreds of workers defy Amazon rules to protest company's climate failures', *Guardian*, 01/28/2020, https://www.theguardian.com/technology/2020/jan/27/amazon-workers-climate-protest

22 Brad Smith, 'Microsoft will be carbon negative by 2030', The Official Microsoft Blog, 01/16/2020, https://blogs.microsoft.com/blog/2020/01/16/microsoft-will-be-carbon-negative-by-2030/

23 Colin Lecher, 'Microsoft employees are protesting the company's "complicity in the climate crisis"', The Verge, 09/19/2020, https://www.theverge.com/2019/9/19/20874081/microsoft-employees-climate-change-letter-protest

24 https://www.schroders.com/en/media-relations/newsroom/all_news_releases/schroders-group-chief-executive-peter-harrison-calls-for-climate-impact-adjusted-profits-at-bloomberg-sustainable-investment-summit/

Chapter 1

1   J. Donald Hughes, 'Ancient Deforestation Revisited', *Journal of the History of Biology*, 44(1), (February 2011), pp. 43–57, https://www.researchgate.net/publication/45407393_Ancient_Deforestation_Revisited

2   https://na.eventscloud.com/file_uploads/03dc178408a7e9a0b3ce03717da11f2d_Biosolidsconftalk-Montgomery.pdf

3   Jeremy Grantham, 'Time to Wake Up', The Oil Drum, 04/29/2011, http://theoildrum.com/node/7853

4   Ethan Shaw, 'Why does the Nile flood each year?' *Sciencing*, 04/25/2017, https://sciencing.com/did-ancient-egyptian-farmers-nile-flooded-18466.html

5   'Land is a critical resource, IPCC report says', IPCC Newsroom, 08/08/2019, https://www.ipcc.ch/2019/08/08/land-is-a-critical-resource_srccl/

6   https://www.ipcc.ch/working-group/wg3/

7   Charles Hall et al., 'Hydrocarbons and the evolution of human culture', *Nature*, Insight commentary, 11/20/2003, https://www.esf.edu/efb/hall/pdfs/OilandCulture.pdf

8   Jeremy Grantham, 'Time to Wake Up', The Oil Drum, 04/29/2011, http://theoildrum.com/node/7853

9   Charles Hall et al., 'Hydrocarbons and the evolution of human culture', *Nature*, Insight commentary, 11/20/2003, https://www.esf.edu/efb/hall/pdfs/OilandCulture.pdf

10 Nicola Jones, 'How to stop data centers from gobbling up the world's electricity', *Nature*, 09/12/2018, https://www.nature.com/articles/d41586-018-06610-y

11 Rebecca Lindsey, 'Climate Change: Atmospheric Carbon Dioxide', NOAA, 08/14/2020, https://www.climate.gov/news-features/understanding-climate/climate-change-atmospheric-carbon-dioxide

12 https://www.breakthroughenergy.org/our-challenge/getting-to-zero

13 'The first big energy shock of the green era', *The Economist*, 10/16/2021, https://www.economist.com/leaders/2021/10/16/the-first-big-energy-shock-of-the-green-era

14 https://www.nationalgeographic.org/encyclopedia/anthropocene/

15 https://unfccc.int/process-and-meetings/the-paris-agreement/the-paris-agreement

16 Hannah Ritchie, 'Emissions by sector', Our World in Data, https://ourworldindata.org/ghg-emissions-by-sector

17 Hannah Ritchie, 'Food production is responsible for one-quarter of the world's greenhouse gas emissions', Our World in Data, 11/06/2019, https://ourworldindata.org/food-ghg-emissions

18 J. Poore et al., 'Reducing food's environmental impacts through producers and consumers', Science, 06/01/2018, https://science.sciencemag.org/content/360/6392/987

19 IPCC Special Report, Climate change and land, https://www.ipcc.ch/srccl/

20 https://ec.europa.eu/food/horizontal-topics/farm-fork-strategy_en

21 'Future of the common agricultural policy', https://ec.europa.eu/info/food-farming-fisheries/key-policies/common-agricultural-policy/future-cap_en

22 https://www.un.org/development/desa/en/news/population/world-population-prospects-2019.html

23 Paul Polman, 'The global challenge of food and nutrition security', Washington Post, 06/17/2012, https://www.washingtonpost.com/opinions/the-global-challenge-of-food-andnutrition-security/2012/06/17/gJQAWse1jV_story.html

24 Anthony Cilluffo, 'World's population is projected to nearly stop growing by the end of the century', Pew Research Center, 06/17/2019, https://www.pewresearch.org/fact-tank/2019/06/17/worlds-population-is-projected-to-nearly-stop-growing-by-the-end-of-the-century/

25 'What is Regenerative Agriculture', 02/17/2016, https://regenerationinternational.org/wp-content/uploads/2017/02/Regen-Ag-Definition-2.23.17-1.pdf

Chapter 2

1 https://oec.world/en/profile/bilateral-product/soybeans/reporter/bra

2 Georgina Rannard, 'COP26: World leaders promise to end deforestation by 2030', BBC News, 11/02/2021, https://www.bbc.co.uk/news/science-environment-59088498

3 'Ethical Consumer: This little piggy doesn't have to go to market', https://cdn.friendsoftheearth.uk/sites/default/files/downloads/ethical-consumer-guide-meat-free-sausages-burgers.pdf

4 Susan Reidy, 'Brazilian soybean production to set record', World-Grain.com, 08/05/2020, https://www.world-grain.com/articles/14060-brazilian-soybean-production-to-set-record

5 Joe Sandler Clarke, 'Brazil pesticide approvals soar as Bolsonaro moves to weaken rules', Greenpeace: Unearthed, 06/12/2019, https://unearthed.greenpeace.org/2019/06/12/jair-bolsonaro-brazil-pesticides/

6 Jenny Gonzales, 'Bolsonaro on the move: International meetings push agribusiness agenda', Mongabay, 03/20/2019, https://news.mongabay.com/2019/03/bolsonaro-on-the-move-international-meetings-push-agribusiness-agenda/

7 'Pesticide intoxication in Brazil and the EU's double standards', Pesticide Action Network Europe, 05/02/2019, https://www.pan-europe.info/press-releases/2019/05/pesticide-intoxication-brazil-and-eus-double-standards

8 Kathleen Wilburn, 'The double bottom line: Profit and social benefit', *Business Horizons*, 57(1), (January–February 2014), pp. 11–20, https://www.sciencedirect.com/science/article/abs/pii/S0007681313001729

9 'Idea: "Triple bottom line"', *The Economist*, 11/17/2009, https://www.economist.com/news/2009/11/17/triple-bottom-line

10 https://www.ifrs.org/groups/international-sustainability-standards-board/

11 Life Cycle Analysis, Science Direct, https://www.sciencedirect.com/topics/earth-and-planetary-sciences/life-cycle-analysis

12 Alan Livsey, 'Accounting needs to be stepped up for climate change costs', *Financial Times*, 03/15/2021, https://www.ft.com/content/92bc2cf3-ef4c-4496-b339-ee178e01d796

13 https://sdgs.un.org/goals

14 https://ec.europa.eu/info/strategy/priorities-2019-2024/european-green-deal_en

15 Neil Hume, 'Anglo American coal spin-off drops on demerger', *Financial Times*, 06/07/2021, https://www.ft.com/content/bd73651f-b9ed-481f-b049-fe768a733d9d

Chapter 3

1 Council on Foundations, 'Foundations Basics', 'What is a Private Foundation?' https://www.cof.org/content/foundation-basics

2 https://www.foundationadvocate.com/foundations-cracked-1-trillion-now-will-people-care/

3 Kerby Meyers, 'The Other 95%: A look at mission-aligned investing', Impactivate, 12/10/2020, https://www.theimpactivate.com/the-other-95-a-look-at-mission-aligned-investing/

4 https://www.mrbf.org/about#content-bar-2e48e372-5a78-4997-8671-60c29286d7ac

5 Kerby Meyers, 'The Other 95%: A look at mission-aligned investing', Impactivate, 12/10/2020, https://www.theimpactivate.com/the-other-95-a-look-at-mission-aligned-investing/

6 JTC Americas Blog, 'The History of Impact Investing: All roads lead to measurement', https://nesfinancial.com/the-history-of-impact-investing-all-roads-lead-to-measurement/

7 Brian Trelstad, 'Impact Investing: A Brief History', 12/15/2016, https://papers.ssrn.com/sol3/papers.cfm?abstract_id=2886088

8 https://www.ashoka.org/en-gb/about-ashoka

Chapter 4

1 Bill Gates, 'My new climate book is finally here', GatesNotes, 02/14/2021, https://www.gatesnotes.com/Energy/My-new-climate-book-is-finally-here

2 *The State of Climate Tech: The next frontier for venture capital*, PwC, https://www.pwc.com/gx/en/services/sustainability/assets/pwc-the-state-of-climate-tech-2020.pdf

3 Corinne Le Quere et al., 'Temporary reduction in daily global CO_2 emissions during the COVID-19 forced confinement', *Nature*

Climate Change, 05/19/2020, https://www.nature.com/articles/
s41558-020-0797-x

4 Alasdair Sandford, 'Coronavirus: Half of humanity now on lockdown
as 90 countries call for confinement', Euronews with AP, AFP,
04/03/2020, https://www.euronews.com/2020/04/02/coronavirus-in-
europe-spain-s-death-toll-hits-10-000-after-record-950-new-deaths-
in-24-hour call for confinement'

5 Alejandra Borunda, 'Plunge in carbon emissions from lockdowns
will not slow climate change', *National Geographic/Science*,
05/20/2020, https://www.nationalgeographic.com/science/article/
plunge-in-carbon-emissions-lockdowns-will-not-slow-climate-change

6 Hannah Ritchie, 'Emissions by sector', Our World in Data, https://
ourworldindata.org/ghg-emissions-by-sector

7 https://www.iea.org/reports/global-energy-review-2020/renewables

8 https://assets.publishing.service.gov.uk/government/uploads/
system/uploads/attachment_data/file/997347/Energy_Trends_
June_2021.pdf

9 Zachary Shahan, 'History of Wind Turbines', Renewable Energy
World, 11/21/2014, https://www.renewableenergyworld.com/
storage/history-of-wind-turbines/#gref

10 https://www.iea.org/data-and-statistics/charts/world-oil-supply-
and-demand-1971-2020

11 https://www.iea.org/reports/natural-gas-information-overview/
demand

12 https://www.cofraholding.com/en/home/

13 'Good Energies invests "green" ahead of the pack', *Wall
Street Journal*, 06/24/2008, https://www.wsj.com/articles/
SB121425575511997973

14 Dr Benjamin Gaddy et al., 'Venture Capital and Cleantech: The
Wrong Model for Clean Energy Innovation', MIT Energy Initiative,
July 2016, https://energy.mit.edu/wp-content/uploads/2016/07/
MITEI-WP-2016-06.pdf

15 Rob Gilhooly, 'Fukushima nuclear accident down to human
factors', *New Scientist*, 07/09/2012, https://www.newscientist.com/

article/dn22031-fukushima-nuclear-accident-down-to-human-factors/

16 Jeremy Hsu, 'Nuclear Power Looks to Regain Its Footing 10 Years after Fukushima', *Scientific American*, 03/09/2021, https://www.scientificamerican.com/article/nuclear-power-looks-to-regain-its-footing-10-years-after-fukushima/

17 Hannah Ritchie and Max Roser, Our World in Data: Nuclear Energy, https://ourworldindata.org/nuclear-energy#putting-death-rates-from-different-energy-sources-in-perspective

18 Steven Pinker, *Rationality: What It Is, Why It Seems Scarce, Why It Matters* (Allen Lane, 2021), p. 121.

19 https://world-nuclear.org/information-library/safety-and-security/safety-of-plants/safety-of-nuclear-power-reactors.aspx

20 Ruby Russell, '40 Years of German Anti-Nuclear action', DW, 06/20/2017, https://www.dw.com/en/40-years-of-german-anti-nuclear-action/g-39477046

21 Germany's election result 2021, *The Economist*, https://www.economist.com/graphic-detail/german-election-results-2021

22 Associated Press, 'Germany votes to end nuclear power by 2022', *Guardian*, 06/30/2011, https://www.theguardian.com/world/2011/jun/30/germany-end-nuclear-power-2022

23 Kerstine Appunn, 'Germany's energy consumption and power mix in charts', Clean Energy Wire, 12/21/2020, https://www.cleanenergywire.org/factsheets/germanys-energy-consumption-and-power-mix-charts

24 Benjamin Wehrmann, 'Bumpy conclusion of Germany's landmark coal act clears way to next energy transition chapters', Clean Energy Wire, 07/03/2020, https://www.cleanenergywire.org/news/bumpy-conclusion-germanys-landmark-coal-act-clears-way-next-energy-transition-chapters

25 Charlotte Nijhuis, 'New EU climate target largely drives coal out of German power market by 2030 – analysis', Clean Energy Wire, 03/17/03, https://www.cleanenergywire.org/news/new-eu-climate-target-largely-drives-coal-out-german-power-market-2030-analysis

26 Reuters staff, 'China's coal consumption seen rising in 2021', Reuters, 03/03/2021, https://www.reuters.com/article/china-coal-idUSL3N2L12A9

27 Reuters, 'U.S. coal-fired electricity generation to rise in 2021, EIA says', 10/18/2021, https://www.reuters.com/business/energy/us-coal-fired-electricity-generation-rise-2021-eia-says-2021-10-18/

28 FT Reporters, 'COP26: what is in the Glasgow Climate Pact?' 11/13/2021, https://www.ft.com/content/3781134d-5567-4eaf-a122-b2595246d4ac

29 https://www.greenpeace.org/international/press-release/50751/cop26-ends-in-glasgow-greenpeace-response/

30 Euronews, 'Macron calls for nuclear "renaissance" to end the (sic) France's reliance on fossil fuels, 11/02/2022, https://www.euronews.com/green/2022/02/11/macron-calls-for-nuclear-renaissance-to-end-the-france-s-reliance-on-fossil-fuels

31 Paul Vieira, 'Canada Embraces Nuclear Energy Expansion to Lower Carbon Emissions', *Wall Street Journal*, 03/03/2021, https://www.wsj.com/articles/canada-embraces-nuclear-energy-expansion-to-lower-carbon-emissions-11614767403

32 Daniel Michaels, 'Mini nuclear reactors offer promise of cheaper, clean power', *Wall Street Journal*, 02/11/2021, https://www.wsj.com/articles/mini-nuclear-reactors-offer-promise-of-cheaper-clean-power-11613055608?mod=article_inline

33 Paul Vieira, 'Canada Embraces Nuclear Energy Expansion to Lower Carbon Emissions', *Wall Street Journal*, 03/03/2021, https://www.wsj.com/articles/canada-embraces-nuclear-energy-expansion-to-lower-carbon-emissions-11614767403

34 'Rolls-Royce gets funding to develop mini nuclear reactors', BBC News: Business, 11/09/2021, https://www.bbc.co.uk/news/business-59212983

35 https://www.terrapower.com/about/

36 Bill Gates, *How to Avoid a Climate Disaster* (Allen Lane, 2021), Chapter 4, 'How to plug in', pp. 86–7.

37 Gates, *How to Avoid a Climate Disaster*, Chapter 4, 'How to plug in', pp.190–91.

38 Harry Kretchmer, 'Renewables are increasingly cheaper than coal', World Economic Forum, 06/23/2020, https://www.weforum.org/agenda/2020/06/renewable-energy-cheaper-coal/

39 Energy Transitions Commission, 'Making Mission Possible: Delivering a Net-Zero Economy', September 2020, https://www.energy-transitions.org/publications/making-mission-possible/

40 *The State of Climate Tech: The next frontier for venture capital*, PwC, https://www.pwc.com/gx/en/services/sustainability/assets/pwc-the-state-of-climate-tech-2020.pdf

41 'Sizing the impact investing market', Global Impact Investing Network, https://thegiin.org/assets/Sizing%20the%20Impact%20Investing%20Market_webfile.pdf

42 John William Olsen, 'Comment: The rise and rise of impact investing', International Investment, 12/17/2020, https://www.internationalinvestment.net/opinion/4025149/comment-rise-rise-impact-investing

43 *The State of Climate Tech 2021: Scaling breakthroughs for net zero*, PwC, https://www.pwc.com/gx/en/services/sustainability/publications/state-of-climate-tech.html

44 *The State of Climate Tech: The next frontier for venture capital*, PwC, https://www.pwc.com/gx/en/services/sustainability/assets/pwc-the-state-of-climate-tech-2020.pdf

45 Gates, *How to Avoid a Climate Disaster*, Chapter 5, 'How we make things', p. 107.

46 'New Report: The building and construction sector can reach net zero carbon emissions by 2050', World Green Building Council, 09/23/2019, https://www.worldgbc.org/news-media/WorldGBC-embodied-carbon-report-published

47 Mike Butcher, '2150 launches with $240M fund to reduce the carbon footprint of the world's growing cities', TechCrunch, 02/23/2021, https://techcrunch.com/2021/02/23/2150-launches-with-281m-fund-to-reduce-the-carbon-footprint-of-the-worlds-growing-cities/

48 Malcolm J. Brandt, 'Energy Use, Sustainability and Waste Treatment', ScienceDirect, https://www.sciencedirect.com/topics/engineering/carbon-accounting

49 https://www.carboncure.com/

50 'How cement may yet help slow global warming', *The Economist*, 11/06/2021, https://www.economist.com/science-and-technology/how-cement-may-yet-help-slow-global-warming/21806083

51 Sonja J. Vermeulen et al., 'Climate Change and Food Systems', 07/30/2012, https://www.annualreviews.org/doi/abs/10.1146/annurev-environ-020411-130608

52 Jacob Bunge, 'How a Billion-dollar Farm-Tech Startup Stumbled, then Revamped', *Wall Street Journal*, 08/22/2021, https://www.wsj.com/articles/how-a-billion-dollar-farm-tech-startup-indigo-stumbled-then-revamped-11629656437

53 https://www.indigoag.com/

54 https://www.crunchbase.com/organization/indigoag

55 https://www.epa.gov/ghgemissions/global-greenhouse-gas-emissions-data

56 https://www.aphea.bio/#overviewanchor

57 'Why product sustainability?', The Sustainability Consortium, https://www.sustainabilityconsortium.org/product-sustainability/

58 https://www.modernmeadow.com/

59 https://www.notpla.com/about/

60 Catherine Clifford, 'Bill Gates expects 8 to 10 Teslas …', CNBC, 10/20/2021, https://www-cnbc-com.cdn.ampproject.org/c/s/www.cnbc.com/amp/2021/10/20/bill-gates-expects-8-to-10-teslas-and-a-google-amazon-and-microsoft.html

61 Deborah Gage, 'The Venture Capital Secret: 3 out of 4 Start-Ups Fail', *Wall Street Journal*, 09/20/2012, https://www.wsj.com/articles/SB10000872396390443720204578004980476429190

Chapter 5

1   'What is Biodiversity?' American Museum of Natural History, https://www.amnh.org/research/center-for-biodiversity-conservation/what-is-biodiversity

2   Edward O. Wilson, 'The Biological Diversity Crisis', *BioScience*, 35(11), (December 1985), pp. 700–06, https://liberiafti.files.wordpress.com/2013/08/wilson_biological-diversity-crisis.pdf

3   Lee Sweetlove, 'Number of species on Earth tagged at 8.7 million', *Nature*, 08/23/2011, https://www.nature.com/articles/news.2011.498

4   UN Report: 'Nature's Dangerous Decline "Unprecedented"; Species Extinction Rates Accelerating', 05/06/2019, https://www.un.org/sustainabledevelopment/blog/2019/05/nature-decline-unprecedented-report/

5   https://www.si.edu/spotlight/buginfo/bugnos

6   Pedro Cardoso et al., 'Scientists' warning to humanity on insect extinctions', *Biological Conservation*, 242, 108426, (February 2020), https://www.sciencedirect.com/science/article/pii/S0006320719317823

7   Esa Valiverronen, 'From "Burning Library" to "Green Medicine": The Role of Metaphors in Communicating Biodiversity', 12/01/2002, https://journals.sagepub.com/doi/abs/10.1177/107554702237848?journalCode=scxb&

8   'Biodiversity and health', 06/03/2015, https://www.who.int/news-room/fact-sheets/detail/biodiversity-and-health

9   'The Bee Cause: Are bees endangered?' Friends of the Earth, https://friendsoftheearth.uk/bees

10 Cara Giaimo, 'Blowing Bubbles to Pollinate Flowers', *New York Times*, 06/17/2020, https://www.nytimes.com/2020/06/17/science/bubbles-pollinating-bees.html

11 Ross Courtney, 'No bees, but a lot of buzz about', Good Fruit Grower, 03/25/2016, https://www.goodfruit.com/no-bees-but-a-lot-of-buzz-about-artificial-pollination-video/

12 Natalie Muller, 'Pollinating by hand: doing bees' work', DW, 07/31/2014, https://www.dw.com/en/pollinating-by-hand-doing-bees-work/a-17822242

13 Xi Yang, 'Soap Bubble Pollination', iScience, 06/17/2020, https://www.cell.com/iscience/fulltext/S2589-0042(20)30373-4?utm_source=EA

14 Issam Ahmed, 'Japanese scientist created soap bubbles that pollinate may help save the world', Breaking Asia, 06/17/2020, https://www.breakingasia.com/news/japanese-scientist-created-soap-bubbles-that-pollinate-plants-may-help-save-the-world/

15 Torsten Kurth, 'The Biodiversity Crisis Is a Business Crisis', BCG, 03/02/2021, https://www.bcg.com/publications/2021/biodiversity-loss-business-implications-responses

16 *Science for Environment Policy*, Issue 529, European Commission, 08/08/2019, https://ec.europa.eu/environment/integration/research/newsalert/pdf/earthworms_soil_quality_pathogen_reduction_529na2_en.pdf

17 Jacqueline L. Stroud, 'Soil health pilot study in England: Outcomes from an on-farm earthworm study', *Plos One*, 02/20/2019, https://journals.plos.org/plosone/article?id=10.1371/journal.pone.0203909

18 Aboulkacem Lemtiri, 'Impacts of earthworms on soil components and dynamics, A review', BASE, 10/09/2012, https://popups.uliege.be/1780-4507/index.php?id=10881

19 William Grimes, 'A Chef in Search of a New Food Chain', *New York Times*, 05/29/2014, https://www.nytimes.com/2014/05/30/books/the-third-plate-by-dan-barber.html

20 'Golf, Pesticides and Organic Practices', Beyond Pesticides, https://www.beyondpesticides.org/resources/golf-and-the-environment/overview

21 'What causes Ocean "Dead Zones"?' *Scientific American*, Sustainability, 09/25/2012, https://www.scientificamerican.com/article/ocean-dead-zones/

22 'What is Over-fishing?' WWF, https://www.worldwildlife.org/threats/overfishing

23 John Roach, 'Seafood May Be Gone by 2048, Study Says', 11/02/2006, https://www.nationalgeographic.com/animals/article/seafood-biodiversity

24 https://www.footprintnetwork.org/our-work/ecological-footprint/

25 https://www.overshootday.org/

26 'Our fertilizer ŸnFrass shows good results on rapeseed, wheat and corn', 10/25/2018, http://www.Ÿnsect.com/en/our-fertilizer-ynfrass-shows-good-performance-on-rapeseed-wheat-corn/

27 'Ÿnsect unveils the results of its insect-based fertilizer – ŸnFrass', 10/25/2018, http://www.Ÿnsect.com/wp-content/uploads/2018/10/PR-Insect-based_fertilizer_Ÿnsect_unveils_the_results_of_its_YnFrass_102518.pdf

28 Tari Gunstone, 'Pesticides and Soil Invertebrates: A Hazard Assessment', *Frontiers in Environmental Science*, 05/04/2021, https://www.frontiersin.org/articles/10.3389/fenvs.2021.643847/full

29 'Pesticides and Soil Health', Center for Biological Diversity', https://www.biologicaldiversity.org/campaigns/pesticides-and-soil-health/

30 'Soils are endangered, but the degradation can be rolled back', UN FAO, 12/04/215, http://www.fao.org/news/story/en/item/357059/icode/

Chapter 6

1 'Sugar 101', American Heart Association, https://www.heart.org/en/healthy-living/healthy-eating/eat-smart/sugar/sugar-101

2 Danny Deza, '16 Most Misleading Food Labels', Health.com, 06/07/2012, https://www.health.com/food/16-most-misleading-food-labels

3 Betty Gold, 'What's the Difference Between Whole Wheat, Whole Grain and Multigrain Bread', Real Simple, 07/14/2020 https://www.realsimple.com/food-recipes/cooking-tips-techniques/whole-wheat-whole-grain-breads-0

4 'Flour Power: Don't know your wholemeal from your wholegrain?' *Men's Health*, 07/23/2007, https://www.menshealth.com/uk/nutrition/a745213/flour-power-80215/

5   'Hidden in Plain Sight', Sugar Science: the Unsweetened Truth, UCSF, https://sugarscience.ucsf.edu/hidden-in-plain-sight/#.YQAcTRoo9p9

6   '61 Names for Sugar', Ohio State University Extension, https://fcs.osu.edu/sites/fcs/files/imce/PDFs/Sixty_One_Names_Sugar_handout.pdf

7   Alex Fox, 'The average American eats 57 pounds of sugar every year', Changing America, The Hill, 11/11/2019, https://thehill.com/changing-america/well-being/longevity/469907-the-average-american-eats-57-pounds-of-sugar-every-year

8   Samir Faruque et al., 'The Dose Makes the Poison: Sugar and Obesity in the United States – a review', NCBI, 01/14/2020, https://www.ncbi.nlm.nih.gov/pmc/articles/PMC6959843/

9   'What you need to know about rationing in the Second World War', Imperial War Museum, https://www.iwm.org.uk/history/what-you-need-to-know-about-rationing-in-the-second-world-war

10 https://www.youtube.com/watch?v=bGr5y2tNoqM

11 'Go to work on an egg', Egg Info: 'Brought to you by British Lion eggs', https://www.egginfo.co.uk/go-work-egg

12 'Organic vs. Free-range – what's the difference?' https://www.soilassociation.org/take-action/organic-living/what-is-organic/organic-eggs/

13 L. A. Horrocks and Y. K. Yeo, 'Health benefits of docosahexaenoic acid (DHA)', *Pharmacological Research*, 40(3), (September 1999), pp.211–25, https://pubmed.ncbi.nlm.nih.gov/10479465/

14 The Nobel Prize in Physiology or Medicine 1982, https://www.nobelprize.org/prizes/medicine/1982/summary/

15 Omega-3 Fatty Acids: An Essential Contribution, Harvard T. H. Chan School of Public Health, https://www.hsph.harvard.edu/nutritionsource/what-should-you-eat/fats-and-cholesterol/types-of-fat/omega-3-fats/

16 Sanjai J. Parikh and Bruce R. James, 'Soil: The Foundation of Agriculture', *Nature Education Knowledge*, 3(10), (2012), p. 2, https://www.nature.com/scitable/knowledge/library/soil-the-foundation-of-agriculture-84224268/

17 Eric Schlosser, *Fast Food Nation*, (Penguin Books, 2002), Chapter 5, 'Why the fries taste good'.

18 Michael Pollan, *The Omnivore's Dilemma* (Bloomsbury, 2006), Chapter 1, 'The Plant: Corn's Conquest, 1. A Naturalist in the Supermarket'.

19 https://international.bleu-blanc-coeur.org/

20 Hannah Landecker, 'Eating as Dialogue, Food as Technology', NOEMA, 06/18/2020, https://www.noemamag.com/eating-as-dialogue-food-as-technology/

21 'Growing at a slower pace, world population is expected to reach 9.7 billion in 2050 and could peak at nearly 11 billion around 2100', UN Department of Economic and Social Affairs, 06/17/2019, WHO News release, 07/15/2019, https://www.un.org/development/desa/en/news/population/world-population-prospects-2019.html

22 'World hunger is still not going down after three years and obesity is still growing – UN Report', https://www.who.int/news/item/15-07-2019-world-hunger-is-still-not-going-down-after-three-years-and-obesity-is-still-growing-un-report

23 Ana Swanson, 'Why trying to help poor countries might actually hurt them', *Washington Post*, 10/13/2015, https://www.washingtonpost.com/news/wonk/wp/2015/10/13/why-trying-to-help-poor-countries-might-actually-hurt-them/

24 'Obesity and overweight – Key facts', WHO, 06/09/2021, https://www.who.int/news-room/fact-sheets/detail/obesity-and-overweight

Chapter 7

1 Compassion in World Farming, https://www.ciwf.org.uk/factory-farming/animal-cruelty/

2 https://animalfreedom.org/english/information/abuses.html

3 'Antibiotics in Our Food', FoodPrint, https://foodprint.org/issues/antibiotics-in-our-food-system/

4 Melinda Wenner Moyer, 'How Drug-Resistant Bacteria Travel from the Farm to your Table', *Scientific American*, 12/01/2016, https://

www.scientificamerican.com/article/how-drug-resistant-bacteria-travel-from-the-farm-to-your-table/

5   https://www.ciwf.org.uk/factory-farming/

6   Yuval Noah Harari, 'Industrial farming is one of the worst crimes in history', *Guardian*, 09/25/2015, https://www.theguardian.com/books/2015/sep/25/industrial-farming-one-worst-crimes-history-ethical-question

7   'Diet, Nutrition, Physical Activity and Cancer: a Global Perspective', World Cancer Research Fund/American Institute for Cancer Research, https://www.wcrf.org/diet-and-cancer/

8   'The Public Health Issues from Our Industrial Food System', FoodPrint, https://foodprint.org/the-total-footprint-of-our-food-system/issues/public-health/

9   K. L. Bassil et al., 'Cancer health effects of pesticides', *Canadian Family Physician*, 53(10), (2007), pp.1704–11, https://www.ncbi.nlm.nih.gov/pmc/articles/PMC2231435/

10 Jonathan Foley, 'It's time to rethink America's corn system', *Scientific American*, 03/05/2021, https://www.scientificamerican.com/article/time-to-rethink-corn/

11 Xavier Poux et al., 'An agro-ecological Europe in 2050: multifunctional agriculture for healthy eating', IDDRI, 18/09/2018, https://www.iddri.org/sites/default/files/PDF/Publications/Catalogue%20Iddri/Etude/201809-ST0918EN-tyfa.pdf

12 '24 billion tons of fertile land lost every year, warns UN Chief...', UN News, Climate and Environment, 06/16/2019, https://news.un.org/en/story/2019/06/1040561

13 Michon Scott, 'Larger-than-average dead zone forecast for Gulf of Mexico in summer 2020', Climate.gov, 07/16/2020, https://www.climate.gov/news-features/event-tracker/larger-average-dead-zone-forecast-gulf-mexico-summer-2020

14 Angelique Chrisafis, '"It can kill you in seconds": the deadly algae on Brittany's beaches', *Guardian*, 09/08/2019, https://www.theguardian.com/environment/2019/sep/08/it-can-kill-you-in-seconds-the-deadly-algae-on-brittanys-beaches

15 'Healthy soils are the basis for healthy food production', 2015 International Year of Soils, http://www.fao.org/soils-2015/news/news-detail/en/c/277682/

16 Leigh Krietsch Boerner, 'Industrial ammonia production emits more CO_2 than any other chemical-making reaction. Chemists want to change that', *Chemical & Engineering News*, 06/15/2019, https://cen.acs.org/environment/green-chemistry/Industrial-ammonia-production-emits-CO2/97/i24

17 Hannah Ritchie, 'How many people does synthetic fertilizer feed?' Our World in Data, 11/07/2017, https://ourworldindata.org/how-many-people-does-synthetic-fertilizer-feed

18 IATP, 'New research shows 50 year binge on chemical fertilisers', 11/01/2021, https://www.iatp.org/new-research-chemical-fertilisers

19 Marcal Capdevila-Cortada, 'Ammonia Synthesis: Electrifying the Haber–Bosch', 12/12/2019, *Nature*, https://www.nature.com/articles/s41929-019-0414-4

20 Sustainable Agriculture vs. Industrial Agriculture, FoodPrint, https://foodprint.org/issues/sustainable-agriculture-vs-industrial-agriculture/

21 http://lib-usda-05.serverfarm.cornell.edu/usda/AgCensusImages/1954/03/04/1087/Table-48.pdf

22 'Farms and Land in Farms', 2017 Summary, USDA, 02/2018, https://www.nass.usda.gov/Publications/Todays_Reports/reports/fnlo0218.pdf

23 'Uneven Ground', Executive Summary: 'In most countries, land inequality is growing', Land Inequality Initiative, https://www.landcoalition.org/en/uneven-ground/executive-summary/

24 Alex Gray, 'This map shows how much each country spends on food', WEF, 12/07/216, https://www.weforum.org/agenda/2016/12/this-map-shows-how-much-each-country-spends-on-food/

25 '10 things you should know about industrial farming', UNEP, 07/20/2020, https://www.unep.org/news-and-stories/story/10-things-you-should-know-about-industrial-farming

26 'World hunger is still not going down after three years and obesity is still growing – UN Report', https://www.who.int/news/item/15-07-

2019-world-hunger-is-still-not-going-down-after-three-years-and-obesity-is-still-growing-un-report

27   Damien Cave, 'Long Slide Looms for World Population, With Sweeping Ramifications', *New York Times*, 22/05/2021, https://www.nytimes.com/2021/05/22/world/global-population-shrinking.html?utm_source=pocket-newtab

28   Florence Chong, 'Agriculture and ESG: Reap what you sow', IPE Real Assets, January/February 2021, https://realassets.ipe.com/forestry-/-agri/agriculture-and-esg-reap-what-you-sow/10050449.article

29   '10 things you should know about industrial farming', UNEP, 07/20/2020, https://www.unep.org/news-and-stories/story/10-things-you-should-know-about-industrial-farming

30   'No time to wait: Securing the future from drug-resistant infections', WHO report to the Secretary-General of the UN, April 2019, https://www.who.int/docs/default-source/documents/no-time-to-wait-securing-the-future-from-drug-resistant-infections-en.pdf?sfvrsn=5b424d7_6

31   Wissem Mnif et al., 'Effect of Endocrine Disruptor Pesticides: A Review', *International Journal of Environmental Research and Public Health*, 8(6), (June 2011), pp. 2265–2303, https://www.ncbi.nlm.nih.gov/pmc/articles/PMC3138025/

32   Javier Mateo-Sagasta, 'Water pollution from agriculture: a global review', FAO/UN, 2017, http://www.iwmi.cgiar.org/Publications/wle/fao/water-pollution-from-agriculture-a-global-review.pdf

33   https://www.youtube.com/watch?v=oLgmk323H6k

34   'Obesity and overweight – Key facts', WHO, 06/09/2021, https://www.who.int/news-room/fact-sheets/detail/obesity-and-overweight

35   Eric Holt-Gimenez, 'We already grow enough food for 10 billion people … and still can't end hunger', *Journal of Sustainable Agriculture*, 36(6), (July 2012), pp. 595–8, https://www.researchgate.net/publication/241746569_We_Already_Grow_Enough_Food_for_10_Billion_People_and_Still_Can%27t_End_Hunger

36   'What is happening to agro-biodiversity?' FAO.org, http://www.fao.org/3/y5609e/y5609e02.htm

37 'Global meat-eating is on the rise, bringing surprising benefits', *The Economist*, 05/04/2019, https://www.economist.com/international/2019/05/04/global-meat-eating-is-on-the-rise-bringing-surprising-benefits

38 Alina Tugend, 'Is the new meat any better than the old meat?' *New York Times*, 09/21/2019, https://www.nytimes.com/2019/09/21/climate/plant-based-meat.html

39 Emma Newburger, 'Beyond Meat uses climate change to market fake meat substitutes. Scientists are cautious', NBC News, 09/02/2019, https://www.cnbc.com/2019/09/02/beyond-meat-uses-climate-change-to-market-fake-meat-substitutes-scientists-are-cautious.html

40 Emily Gelsomin, 'Impossible and Beyond: How healthy are these meatless burgers?' Harvard Health Publishing, 08/15/2019, https://www.health.harvard.edu/blog/impossible-and-beyond-how-healthy-are-these-meatless-burgers-2019081517448

41 Gary Kleppel, *The Emergent Agriculture: Farming, Sustainability and the Return of the Local Economy* (New Society Publishers, 2014), Chapter 5, 'Sustainable Meat – A Contradiction in Terms?' p. 45.

42 Rodale Institute, 'Crop Rotations', https://rodaleinstitute.org/why-organic/organic-farming-practices/crop-rotations/

43 Janet K. Jansson, 'Soil microbiomes and climate change', *Nature*, 10/04/2019, https://www.nature.com/articles/s41579-019-0265-7

44 Martina Koberl et al., 'Unraveling the Complexity of Soil Microbiomes in a Large-Scale Study ...', *Frontiers in Microbiology*, 05/25/2020, https://www.frontiersin.org/articles/10.3389/fmicb.2020.01052/full

45 https://vib.be/research-areas/plant-biology-labs

46 https://vib.be/grand-challenges-program/soy-flanders

47 https://x.company/projects/mineral/

48 John Warren, 'Why do we consume only a tiny fraction of the world's edible plants?' World Economic Forum/Project Syndicate, 01/15/2016, https://www.weforum.org/agenda/2016/01/why-do-we-consume-only-a-tiny-fraction-of-the-world-s-edible-plants

49 https://astanor.com/cases/maggrow/

50 https://www.maggrow.com/our-technology

Chapter 8

1 *Village Fair at Hoboken* (*c.*1559), attributed to Franz Hogenberg after Pieter Bruegel the Elder, National Gallery of Art, Washington DC, https://www.nga.gov/collection/art-object-page.47609.html

2 Peggy Lowe, 'Everything but the squeal: How the hog industry cuts food waste', NPR, The Salt, 09/29/2014, https://www.npr.org/sections/thesalt/2014/09/29/351495505/everything-but-the-squeal-how-the-hog-industry-cuts-food-waste?t=1627641519721

3 https://www.goodfoodrevolution.com/mark-essig-pig-historian/

4 'Famines through History', 03/08/2004, https://www.thefreelibrary.com/Famines+through+history.-a0114325996

5 Book review of Peter Garnsey, *Famine and Food Supply in the Graeco-Roman World*, UNRV Roman History, https://www.unrv.com/book-review/famine-food-supply.php

6 *The Oxford Encyclopedia of Ancient Greece and Rome*, co-search?btog=chap&q0=blood+pudding&source=%2F10.1093%-2Facref%2F9780195170726.001.0001%2Facref-9780195170726

7 'Food loss and food waste', FAO of the UN, http://www.fao.org/food-loss-and-food-waste/flw-data)

8 'Worldwide food waste', UNEP, https://www.unep.org/thinkeatsave/get-informed/worldwide-food-waste

9 Sustainability Pathways: 'Food Waste Footprint', FAO of the UN, http://www.fao.org/nr/sustainability/food-loss-and-waste/en/

10 https://databank.worldbank.org/data/download/GDP.pdf

11 https://www.nationalgeographic.com/magazine/article/plastic-planet-waste-pollution-trash-crisis

12 'Our planet is drowning in plastic pollution – it's time for change!' UNEP, https://www.unep.org/interactive/beat-plastic-pollution/

13 https://www.ted.com/talks/kim_ragaert_plastics_rehab

14 https://assets.publishing.service.gov.uk/government/uploads/system/ uploads/attachment_data/file/291023/scho0711buan-e-e.pdf

15 Elizabeth Cline, 'Where does discarded clothing go?' *The Atlantic*, 07/18/2014, https://www.theatlantic.com/business/ archive/2014/07/where-does-discarded-clothing-go/374613/

16 https://www.greenmatch.co.uk/blog/2016/08/fast-fashion-the-second-largest-polluter-in-the-world

17 'Toxic Threads: The Big Fashion Stitch-Up', Greenpeace International, 11/2012, https://www.greenpeace.org/static/planet4-international-stateless/2012/11/317d2d47-toxicthreads01.pdf

18 Andrea Newell, 'Quenching Cotton's Thirst: Reducing the Use of Water in the Cotton Lifecycle', Triple Pundit, 02/23/2016, https:// www.triplepundit.com/story/2016/quenching-cottons-thirst-reducing-use-water-cotton-lifecycle/57196

19 Mark Anthony Browne, 'Accumulations of microplastic on shorelines worldwide', Environmental Science & Technology, 09/14/2011, https://www.plasticsoupfoundation.org/wp-content/ uploads/2015/03/Browne_2011-EST-Accumulation_of_microplastics-worldwide-sources-sinks.pdf

20 'Synthetic fibres used in 72% of clothing items can sit in landfills for 200 years', Sustainable Fashion.Earth, 04/25/2019, https://www. sustainablefashion.earth/type/water/synthetic-fibres-used-in-72-clothing-items-can-sit-in-landfills-for-200-years/

21 'How Much Do Our Wardrobes Cost to the Environment?' The World Bank, 09/23/2019, https://www.worldbank.org/en/news/ feature/2019/09/23/costo-moda-medio-ambiente

22 Anne-Sophie Brandlin, 'Why cheap groceries will hurt us all in the long run', Deutsche Welle, 09/14/2020, https://www.dw.com/en/ food-sustainability-organic-discounter-cheap-environmental-costs-prices-factory-farming/a-54919142

23 https://ec.europa.eu/eurostat/web/products-eurostat-news/-/ DDN-20181204-1

24 'Food waste falls by 7% per person in three years', WRAP press release, 01/24/2020, https://wrap.org.uk/media-centre/press-releases/food-waste-falls-7-person-three-years

25 https://olioex.com/about/

26 https://olioex.com/about/our-impact/

27 https://whywaste.com/

28 https://karma.life/about

29 https://toogoodtogo.org/en

30 https://toogoodtogo.org/en/movement/politics/date-labelling-campaigns

31 https://www.afresh.com/

32 https://www.shelfengine.com/

33 https://www.apeel.com/

34 Cutin, ScienceDirect, Advances in agronomy, 2017, https://www.sciencedirect.com/topics/agricultural-and-biological-sciences/cutin

35 Apeel Team, 'Accelerating Innovation to Further our Mission', 18/9/2021, https://blog.apeelsciences.com/accelerating-innovation-to-further-our-mission

36 https://www.crunchbase.com/organization/apeel-sciences

37 https://assets.website-files.com/5f31bfa796b7553c22964294/5f4ea7f01180293d8107723e_AvoApeel-SustainabilityScorecard-Avocado-ENG-AUG2020-digital.pdf

38 https://www.xampla.com/

39 https://www.seariousbusiness.com/

40 https://www.waes.co/pages/about

41 https://calyxia.com/about-us

42 https://biorius.com/regulatory/future-restriction-of-microplastics-in-cosmetic-products/

43 https://eeb.org/eu-moves-to-ban-microplastics-in-most-products/

44 Natasha Lomas, 'Calyxia bags $17.6m to tackle the global microplastics problem', TechCrunch, 09/22/2021, https://

techcrunch.com/2021/09/22/calyxia-bags-17-6m-to-tackle-the-global-microplastics-problem/

Chapter 9

1 https://www.princeofwales.gov.uk/speech/speech-hrh-prince-wales-future-food-conference-georgetown-university-washington-dc

2 Lisa Walden, 'The surprising thing Prince Charles does when planting trees', *Country Living*, 12/15/2020, https://www.countryliving.com/uk/homes-interiors/gardens/a34971782/prince-charles-ritual-planting-trees/

3 Charles, Prince of Wales, 'Small farms have a huge role to play in our sustainable future', *Guardian*, 05/23/2021, https://www.theguardian.com/commentisfree/2021/may/23/small-farms-huge-role-sustainable-future-prince-charles

4 https://soylent.com/

5 Brian X. Chen, 'In busy Silicon Valley, Protein Powder Is in Demand', *New York Times*, 05/25/2015, https://www.nytimes.com/2015/05/25/technology/in-busy-silicon-valley-protein-powder-is-in-demand.html?_r=0

6 Elizabeth Segran, 'Soylent is basically SlimFast for men', *Fast Company*, 06/21/2016, https://www.fastcompany.com/4011274/soylent-is-basically-slimfast-for-men

7 Beth Kowitt, 'Soylent, once the beverage of tech bros, finds a new audience', *Fortune*, 07/28/2021, https://fortune-com.cdn.ampproject.org/c/s/fortune.com/2021/07/28/soylent-retail-nutrition-rite-aid-walmart/amp/

8 'Carving up the alternative meat market', Barclays, Insights, 08/19/2019, https://www.investmentbank.barclays.com/our-insights/carving-up-the-alternative-meat-market.html

9 Emiko Terazono, 'Lab-grown chicken start-up slashes production costs', *Financial Times*, 05/06/2021, https://www.ft.com/content/ae4dd452-f3e0-4a38-a29d-3516c5280bc7

10 Martine Paris, 'Future Meat Raises $347 Million to Make Cell-Grown Meat in U.S.', Bloomberg, 12/17/2021, https://www.bloomberg.

com/news/articles/2021-12-17/future-meat-raises-347-million-to-make-cell-grown-meat-in-u-s

11 https://mosameat.com/growing-beef

12 https://www.upsidefoods.com/about-us

13 Karen Gilchrist, 'This multibillion-dollar company is selling lab-grown chicken in a world first', CNBC, 03/01/2021, https://www.cnbc.com/2021/03/01/eat-just-good-meat-sells-lab-grown-cultured-chicken-in-world-first.html

14 https://shiokmeats.com/faq/

15 https://depts.washington.edu/ceeh/downloads/FF_Microbiome.pdf

16 https://depts.washington.edu/ceeh/downloads/FF_Microbiome.pdf

17 Cassandra Willyard, 'How gut microbes could drive brain disorders', Nature, News Feature, 02/03/2021, https://www.nature.com/articles/d41586-021-00260-3

18 Marwa Azab, 'Gut Bacteria Can Influence Your Mood, Thoughts and Brain', Psychology Today, 08/07/2019, https://www.psychologytoday.com/gb/blog/neuroscience-in-everyday-life/201908/gut-bacteria-can-influence-your-mood-thoughts-and-brain

19 Peter J. Turnbaugh et al., 'A core gut microbiome in obese and lean twins', Nature, 457 (2009), pp.480–4, https://www.nature.com/articles/nature07540

20 Michelle Beaumont et al., 'Heritable components of the human fecal microbiome are associated with visceral fat', Genome Biology, 17, 189 (2016), https://genomebiology.biomedcentral.com/articles/10.1186/s13059-016-1052-7

21 'Abdominal fat and what to do about it', Harvard Health Publishing, 06/25/2019, https://www.health.harvard.edu/staying-healthy/abdominal-fat-and-what-to-do-about-it

22 'Make-up of gut microbiome may influence COVID-19 severity and immune response', BMJ, Newsroom, 01/11/2021, https://www.bmj.com/company/newsroom/make-up-of-gut-microbiome-may-influence-covid-19-severity-and-immune-response/

23 Yun Kit Yeoh et al., 'Gut microbial composition reflects disease severity and dysfunctional immune responses in patients with COVID-19', *Gut*, 70 (2021), pp.698–706, https://gut.bmj.com/content/70/4/698

24 Hannah Landecker, 'Eating as Dialogue, Food as Technology', NOEMA, 06/18/2020, https://www.noemamag.com/eating-as-dialogue-food-as-technology/

25 'Pioneering cellular nutrition for healthy aging', Nestlé, 10/14/2020, https://www.nestle.com/randd/news/allnews/pioneering-cellular-nutrition-healthy-aging

26 Saabira Chaudhuri, 'Older shoppers are the hot new thing for consumer brands', *Wall Street Journal*, 01/30/2021, https://www.wsj.com/articles/older-shoppers-are-the-hot-new-thing-for-consumer-brands-11612002644

Coda

1 Salem Gebrekidan, 'The Money Farmers: How Oligarchs and Populists Milk the E.U. for millions', *New York Times*, 11/03/2019, https://www.nytimes.com/2019/11/03/world/europe/eu-farm-subsidy-hungary.html

2 'Political agreement on new Common Agricultural Policy: fairer, greener, more flexible', European Commission press release, 06/25/2021, https://ec.europa.eu/commission/presscorner/detail/en/IP_21_2711

3 Murray W. Scown, 'Billions in Misspent EU Agricultural Subsidies Could Support the Sustainable Development Goals', *One Earth*, 3(2), (21 August 2020), pp.173–5, https://www.sciencedirect.com/science/article/pii/S2590332220303559

4 https://vivonsenforme.org/

5 https://nutriscore.colruytgroup.com/colruytgroup/en/about-nutri-score/

6 https://yuka.io/en/

7 https://corporate.colruytgroup.com/corp/static/assets/eco/ECOSCORE_EN.pdf

8   https://contxto.com/en/chile/ok-to-shop-application-finding-right-food-supermarket/

9   Sarah Boseley, 'Chile's drastic anti-obesity measures cut sugary drink sales by 23%', *Guardian*, 02/11/2020, https://www.theguardian.com/world/2020/feb/11/chiles-drastic-anti-obesity-measures-cut-sugary-drink-sales-by-23

10 'Big opportunities for small firms: government set to spend £1 in every £3 with small businesses', Cabinet Office, Crown Commercial Service, 08/27/2015, https://www.gov.uk/government/news/big-opportunities-for-small-firms-government-set-to-spend-1-in-every-3-with-small-businesses

11 https://ec.europa.eu/info/business-economy-euro/banking-and-finance/sustainable-finance/overview-sustainable-finance_en

12 https://ec.europa.eu/programmes/horizon2020/what-horizon-2020

13 https://miimosa.com/fr

14 https://be.lita.co/en

Acknowledgements

This book is the result of almost two decades of a learning journey across the world and the progressive crystallization of ideas that would not have been possible without the contribution of dozens of conversations and experimentations with tens of exceptional people whom I would like to acknowledge.

I am very thankful for my very long-time friendship and working relationship with Charly Kleissner and his wife Lisa with whom I have shared together many entrepreneurial adventures in Silicon Valley followed by our pioneering work in impact investing ... even before it was called impact investing. Also to Guillaume Taylor with whom I co-founded Quadia, one of the first impact investing financial firms, and to Peter Wheeler, long-time friend and impact travelling companion at Social Impact and at Quadia.

Some very special thanks to my impact investing business partners at Astanor Ventures, Kathleen Merrigan, Christina Ulardic, Hendrik van Asbroeck, David Barber, George Powlick and Hans Marteau, all believers in the urgent need to measure financial results with an impact lens. A special mention to my Astanor co-founder and long-time partner George Coelho for having believed since day one in my vision for a regenerative agrifood system and for Emmanuel Faber for his early engagement as a sustainable business activist who inspired me and for our fascinating exchanges on impact creation and measurement over the past few years, which ended up in us becoming business partners at Astanor. Thank you, Giles Gibbons, for sharing with me during intense brainstorming sessions your experiences and visions in the world of food services. And to my trusted advisor Khoi Tu, a most brilliant person who believed early in my capacity to assemble the Astanor team around its mission to leverage nature with technology for enabling a sustainable future of food. Finally, my heartfelt gratitude to Diane and Charles Adriaenssen and to Renée and Hans Wackwitz for their early support for Astanor. They became much more than friends and investors on this journey into Impact Investing.

Not forgetting my old-time colleagues Christian Reitberger and Frank Boehnke, both visionary venture investors and personal actors of sustainability projects, from energy to farming, who supported my initial forays in the agrifood tech sector.

Thank you to those who alerted me early about the dismal state of the soil everywhere but also about the emerging solution called regenerative agriculture, starting with Chuck de Liedekerke and Nicolas Verschuere, the founders of Soil Capital, and then those who are practising it with undying passion, infinite patience and brilliance: Charlotte Horton at Potentino in Italy, and in France, Pierre Breton in Bourgueuil, Gerard Sage in L'Île d'Yeu and Barbara de Nicolai in Le Lude, among several others who will recognize themselves.

I was extremely fortunate to cross paths and sustain deep exchanges and friendship with several chefs extraordinaire who have been reinventing the future of food, one delicious plate at a time, with local, seasonal and sustainably grown ingredients. Guy Savoy in Paris gave me my first shockingly good experience of sustainable greatness in food and has continued to do so every year since 1998. Olivier Roelinger in Brittany and Pierre Gagnaire in Paris pursued my introduction to great cuisine with the highest respect for the ingredients. Chef John-Paul Carmona brought his magic to many of my personal food projects, from foraging in L'Île d'Yeu in France or on the West Coast of Mexico to preparing memorable feasts for large groups with local, seasonal produce. A big acknowledgement goes to Rene Redzepi, who single-handedly transformed the Nordic cuisine with Noma and went on to inspire a generation of chefs world-wide to rethink the meaning of food and then inspired me to seek solutions to rethink the world of food. Alex Atala in San Paolo, Magnus Nielssen in Åre in the north of Sweden, Bruno Verjus in Paris , David Zilber and Matt Orlando in Copenhagen then all showed me a glimpse of how the future of food could combine sustainability and deliciousness.

Finally, Jamie Oliver will always have a special place in my heart and soul, having entrusted me to chair JOFF, his foundation for food education, where we attempted, and succeeded, at educating scores of children and families about the perils of bad food and the joys and easiness of cooking from scratch.

Words can't capture all my gratitude for the brilliant minds and amazing scientists, technologists and entrepreneurs that provided so many insights and so much content for this book:

Professor David Montgomery, Dr Anne Bikle and Professor Karine Clément for their inspiring work in the microbiome of the soil and the microbiome of humans – and for our late-night conversations in the Loire Valley about their resemblance.

Pierre Weill, agronomist, entrepreneur, author and tireless activist of sustainable agriculture and food as medicine for his work that inspired me early on.

The very inspiring entrepreneurs and engineers with whom I have had the privilege to work closely at Astanor: Antoine Hubert and Jean-Gabriel Levon (Ÿnsect in Paris), Osnat Michaeli and Erez Galonska (Infarm in Berlin), Michael Heinrich (Garten in San Francisco), James Roger (Apeel in Santa Barbara), Lars Williams and Mark-Emil Hermansen (Empirical Spirit in Copenhagen) and especially those whose stories have made this book more real: Andras Forgacs (Modern Meadow in New York), Tessa Clarke (OLIO in London) and Pierre Paslier and Rodrigo García González (Notpla in London).

And to the founders of DASRA in Mumbai, Deval Sanghavi and Neera Nundi, with whom we worked on some of the most impactful projects at scale, ranging from access to sustainable agriculture technology to waste management and recycling.

I offer my warmest gratitude to my wife, Sophie, and our children, Alix, Paul and Charles, for their patience, encouragement and love all through my many years of intense professional activity, not limited to but including this book project.

Finally, this book would not exist without the tireless support of James Silver who has helped me whenever the engineer in me was struggling to find the right words to express my ideas clearly and succinctly. And a huge thank you to the friends and partners who reviewed the manuscript, and especially to the very sharp minds of two impact investing specialists who spent precious weekends reviewing entire chapters: Leslie Kapin at Astanor Ventures and Lisa Schmitt at Kreditanstalt für Wiederaufbau (the German Federal Development Bank).

About the author

Eric Archambeau is an engineer, former Silicon Valley entrepreneur, venture capitalist and the co-founder of Astanor Ventures, an impact-led venture capital firm focusing on technology-enabled start-up companies in the regenerative agriculture and sustainable food sectors, with investments in companies such as Apeel Sciences, Empirical Spirit, Infarm, Modern Meadow, Monarch Tractors, Plantible, Smallhold and Ÿnsect.

Before Astanor, Eric had been a business angel, venture capital investor, member of the board of directors and mentor to many founders of disruptive technology companies across the US, the UK and the EU, including, among others, eGroups (Yahoo groups), Flutter Entertainment PLC, PriceMinister (now Rakuten), XING, Spotify, Threads Styling, Freenow, Onfido, Peakon and Pirate Studios.

Over the past two decades, he has also worked as investor and mentor with social entrepreneurs, addressing key social and environmental challenges, including Maven Clinic, a digital health clinic for women, in New York, and DASRA-Social Impact, a social impact accelerator in Mumbai. Eric was an early supporter of social entrepreneurship network Ashoka in Europe, and a founding member of the Ashoka Support Network.

Eric has also lectured at INSEAD, where he founded the social entrepreneurship programme, and served as Global Chairman of the Jamie Oliver Food Foundation, providing food education for children across the world.

Index

Page numbers in **bold** indicate figures.